THE UFO PEOPLE:

A CURIOUS CULTURE

THE UFO PEOPLE:

A CURIOUS CULTURE

BY

MJ BANIAS

www.augustnightbooks.com

In 1973, Dr. J. Allen Hynek, who is featured in the photograph, travelled to Piedmont, Missouri to investigate a string of UFO sightings. Hynek's friend, Ted Phillips, took this famous picture of him in front of the Waltrip Motel sign.

Thank you to Ted and Ginger Phillips for allowing me to use this photograph.

For Laura,
always.

About the author

MJ Banias is an educator and writer. His popular blog, *Terra Obscura*, critically examines how philosophy and culture affect society's understanding of anomalous phenomena, including UFOs. He has been interviewed on many podcasts and radio shows. His work has been featured in Fortean Times Magazine, *FATE Magazine* and in the book *UFOs: Reframing the Debate* (White Crow Books). He is a regular contributor to the website, *Mysterious Universe* and hosts his own YouTube channel. He lives in Canada with his wife, two children, and a massive cat.

PRAISE FOR

The UFO People

"MJ Banias' *The UFO People: A Curious Culture* is an alluring and captivating exploration not so much of the UFO phenomenon as the people who become obsessed with it. The author's training in critical theory and philosophy informs his discussion of what can, and what cannot, be known about the phenomenon. He has done his homework, interviewing some of the major scientific players in the field, such as Dr. Hal Puthoff, Dr. Garry Nolan, and Dr. Christopher Greene, among others.

Banias identifies that UFO phenomena are so many things that the word "UFO" is practically meaningless, while also revealing that the "believers" and scientists who study these phenomena are as interesting as the phenomena themselves.

Banias is the first UFO researcher, to my knowledge, to tackle the ontological reality of something that doesn't *seem* to exist. Instead of attempting to identify the "hardware," the nuts and bolts of crafts, etc., Banias tackles the phenomenon from a macro-perspective and situates it within the collective human psyche. *The UFO People* is one of the best books to come along that offers a new theoretical framework for this confusing, but nonetheless captivating, topic. For anyone interested in social history, UFOs, or just looking for an interesting and engaging read, this is their book."

~DIANA WALSH PASULKA, PROFESSOR,
UNIVERSITY OF NORTH CAROLINA WILMINGTON
CHAIR, DEPARTMENT OF PHILOSOPHY AND RELIGION
AUTHOR, *AMERICAN COSMIC: UFOs, RELIGION, TECHNOLOGY*

"MJ Banias brings a different look at ufology and ufologists, covering the waterfront from his personal investigation of UFO cases to his conversations with some of the most controversial figures in the field. But beyond that, he calls on his background in philosophy to ask deep questions about the UFO phenomenon and the UFO community itself, wondering if the marginalized "ghosts" of aliens and paranormal denizens are any more or less "real" than other beliefs in modern society, deconstructing what we know, don't know, and think we know about UFOs."

~CHRIS RUTKOWSKI,
SCIENCE WRITER AND FORTEAN SCHOLAR,
AUTHOR OF TEN BOOKS ON ECLECTIC PHENOMENA AND
CO-AUTHOR OF *WHEN THEY APPEARED: FALCON LAKE 1967:
THE INSIDE STORY OF A CLOSE ENCOUNTER.*

CONTENTS

ACKNOWLEDGEMENTS

~

Undoubtedly, I have overlooked many people. Time has a funny way of helping you forget things, so I will begin by thanking all of you inside and outside of the UFO community who took part in this strange adventure with me. While your name may have been missed here in text, your contribution nonetheless was appreciated and required for this book to be completed successfully.

Thank you to my publisher, especially Robbie Graham, who saw something in me and decided to give me a chance. Thank you for the countless hours, emails, and conversations that made this book happen. Thank you to Allison Jornlin for your contribution to this book. Your dedication to your craft is inspiring. Know that your work in the field of Fortean research is ahead of the curve, and that many look to your work with admiration.

Thank you to Barry Greenwood who co-wrote an essay for this book and took a chance by putting his name into a work written by an untested author. Thank you to Paul Dean who took this step with Barry, but also spent many late Australian nights speaking with me over the phone. Your wisdom and knowledge regarding the history of the UFO enigma is second to none. Many aspects of this book, that stuff in-between the written lines, are built upon the conversations and endless sharing of information contributed by Paul. If you are reading this, Paul, you are a gem, and one helluva friend.

Thank you to Jesse Laing for coming along on this wild ride, and all of those evening beers at The Common.

Thank you to Amy "A.J." McCormick who shared with me some of the deepest aspects of her life. Thank you for your writing and your stories. Thank you for the conversations, the quick chats and the friendship. I hope this book convinces you that you need not be afraid because you are not alone, and that you find peace in embracing your place in this complex story.

Thank you to Richard Doty who sat patiently through my countless questions. At times, I have little doubt that I was highly annoying. Thank you for indulging me.

Thank you to Dr. Garry Nolan, Dr. Kit Green, and Dr. Hal Puthoff for speaking with me on multiple occasions. Your insights into the UFO subculture were enlightening and I wish you all nothing but the best of luck in your respective projects. Keep that ball moving forward.

Thank you to Chris Rutkowski who decided that I ought to get myself into this mess. I did. This is all your fault, but it has been a fun ride. Thank you for showing me the door and shoving me through it.

Thank you to Ryan Sprague, Jason McClellan, Maureen Elsberry, Mike Damante, Chase Kloetzke, Sue Demeter-St. Clair, Diana Pasulka, Erica Lukes, Isaac Koi, Jane Kyle, Cheryl Costa, Scott Browne, David Stinnett, Ted and Ginger Phillips, Saiko (whoever you are...), Shannon Legro, Alison Kruse, Micah Hanks, George P. Hansen, Greg Bishop, Jeff Ritzman, and Miguel Romero. Books are a sum of their parts, and you, in some way, contributed to the development and the process, which made this possible. Your insight and ideas are inspiring.

Thank you to Colin, Michael, Tina, Christina and (of course) Anthony, for the countless bonfire debates, and to Ron and Christine for the discussions around the dinner table (and all the free suppers). Your genuine interest in my endeavours has helped me to undertake this project.

Thank you to my parents, Ivan and Olga, who let their impressionable young son stay up way too late to watch *The Outer Limits and The X-Files*. Moreover, thank you for your unending support, your love, and making me the person I am today.

Thank you to Cecily and Simon who remind me on a daily basis that life through the eyes of a child is significantly more real and magical than that of any adult. You two show me a world where anything is possible.

Thank you to my wife, Laura who kept me grounded when this project began to pull me away. You have kept me sane. Thank you for being my muse, my proof-reader, and my sounding board. You are my love, my best friend, and thank you for helping me to pursue this insane dream.

Finally, thank you to all of you who were purposefully unmentioned. Whether you wish to continue to work and live in peace or want to avoid conflict, your quiet and anonymous contributions to this book have provided true depth and breadth to the overall puzzle. May you find what you seek.

PROLOGUE

Fire, Whiskey, and UFOs

In the Canadian prairies, the sky rolls on forever, and, on clear nights, out in the woods where my family and I often come to sit, have fires, and drink scotch, I often look up and see nothing but the black of deep space and the millions of twinkling stars shining their light upon the Earth.

One night, many years ago, I was sitting around one such fire. Anthony, my brother-in-law, handed me a glass of scotch, Laphroaig, and definitely not my first that night. I looked up at the sky and saw a point of light, distant and tiny, slowly move across my field of view. It was the International Space Station.

"It's wild to think that they are up there," I said, out loud, mostly to myself.

"Pops saw one once."

"Saw what?" I was confused.

"A UFO. Middle of the day. You should ask him."

"I didn't see a UFO," I responded. I knew what it was. It was the space station, but it was too late. We were already on the subject.

"Your dad saw a UFO?"

"When he was young. Eighteen or nineteen," Anthony looked up at the sky.

"What did it look like?" I was intrigued. A little family secret I had never known.

"A rectangle or square. You'll have to ask him. Do you think we are alone? Look at all that light."

I looked up, "I doubt we are alone. I don't really believe they are coming here, though."

"Who knows," Anthony replied. "But everyone believes in something. Why not that?"

Great insight tends to happen around an open fire in the middle of the forest, and usually a good glass of whiskey tends to get itself involved somehow. We all believe in something. However, perhaps *believe* is not the correct word. Maybe *pursue* is more apt. Whether it is God, or love, or justice, or karma, or happiness or anything else for that matter, we all have a tendency to pursue something or someone. We have no explanation for why; we simply do. We become wanderers, ghosts, drifting from point-to-point, seeking out that which we think will save us. We try to understand why we believe it, why we dare to pursue something that nearly always seems unreachable. For one curious and particular group, a subculture dwelling on the fringe, that eternal pursuit forms around one curious phenomenon: UFOs. This unknowable specter creates truth and myth wherever it goes; it forms identities and ideologies, and, more importantly, it changes the landscape of the self.

~

We didn't know it then, but Anthony hit upon an idea that would push me down a path towards exploring one of the world's most interesting groups of people, and even becoming one of them myself.

This is not a book about UFOs. It is a book about people.

INTRODUCTION

~

This book hinges upon a massive *I don't know*. I don't know what *Unidentified Flying Objects* are. I don't know if extraterrestrials or flying saucers are visiting Earth. I don't know if abductions are real. I don't know if people can channel strange entities from parallel dimensions. A great many people I have spoken to say that these things are real and happening. Perhaps they are. To move forward then, I must check my bias; I must remain agnostic and not assume that UFOs or enigmatic interdimensional alien entities are the stuff of fiction. I suppose I have to get comfortable in this dark chasm, this gap, this *I don't know*.

Here are two things I do know, however. First, anyone who suggests that they understand and *know* what the UFO phenomenon is or makes claims regarding it, which they assert to be true, is probably trying to sell something or garner some attention. It is possible that they may also be delusional, or, at the very least, lack insight or the ability to think critically. This applies to the most ardent overzealous believer and closed-minded skeptic. I appreciate that this may come off as overbearing and highly critical. I hope it does. The last thing any good discourse or debate needs is a lazy individual too caught up in his or her own rigid fantasy. Second, according to hundreds-of-thousands of reports across the globe and going back millennia, we have encountered things that we could not explain. Does this mean that every single unexplainable event is a message from spirits, alien beings, or mystical creatures? No. Does this mean that every single sighting of a UFO or extraterrestrial entity is otherworldly in nature? No. Just because someone saw *something* doesn't mean that it is real or true. Lies and delusion are also an authentic phenomenon. However, for many anomalous and strange things, we have become clever enough to find answers and fit them into our understanding of the world. We know that bubonic plague is not caused by evil spirits and that lightning is not the wrath of a vengeful god. That being said, there are still many things that escape our explanation. Many mysteries remain, and strange anomalies continue to haunt us. Indeed, one day, many more of these odd events will be explainable as our ability to learn, grow and understand changes. We will continue to develop. However, until those curious and odd phenomena become reduced to basic provable facts which can be known, many academic authorities or elite institutions oddly continue to suggest that anomalies do not happen. They are tricks of the mind or errors in data collection. While it is true that errors happen, can those same people claim that nothing is currently outside of human knowledge? Have we learned all there is to learn? The more we stamp our feet saying that something cannot be, yet have no evidence to prove that to be the case, the more we ought to realize that we are simple toddlers smashing away at a puzzle piece that simply refuses to fit properly.

We must look at this puzzle differently. I will begin by making two simple assumptions for the purpose of this book.

First, strange unexplainable things happen. That's it. Nothing more. A little open-mindedness isn't scary, is it?

Second, the term "UFO phenomenon" is not clearly definable. In his book, *The Super Natural: A New Vision of the Unexplained*, author and academic Jeffrey Kripal compares the "UFO phenomenon" to "a wastebasket problem." He writes:

> [the] UFO phenomenon is not a single thing. It is a broad set of things that are constantly being confused and mixed up.[1]

We tend to hold assumptions concerning exactly what we believe the UFO phenomenon to encompass and toss all those assumptions into the wastebasket, creating a chaotic mix of ideas, which have little rhyme or reason to be together. During my time spent digging into both the community and the phenomenon, I began to wonder what exactly does "UFO phenomenon" include? Do we lump alien abductions and extraterrestrial contact in with seeing strange lights and unknown objects

---

[1]   Kripal, Jeffrey and Strieber, Whitley. *The Super Natural: A New Vision of the Unexplained*. Penguin. New York. 2016, 9.

in the sky? The channeling of interdimensional entities or spirits, and even poltergeist activity, often accompany UFO sightings, as do sightings of Sasquatch. Are these all part of the UFO enigma? While the term "UFO" itself began as an American Cold War military response to "foo fighters" and flying saucers, it has often been mingled with parapsychological phenomena such as remote viewing and telepathy. How about ancient sightings and reports of fairies, goblins, and elves? Various other modern creatures like the Mothman and the Flatwoods Monster also have connections to the UFO phenomenon. How about New Age mystical beliefs, UFO cults, demonology, secret military black aerospace projects, seeing ghosts of deceased loved ones, and near-death experiences? More importantly, do all the people who study and engage in discourse regarding these various phenomena fall into the UFO subculture? Simply put, the UFO phenomenon and community have fingers in a lot of pies.

Since it is impossible to come to any consensus regarding what is meant by "UFO phenomenon," can we actually come to a formal definition of who makes up the subculture? Is the UFO community simply those who chase odd lights in the sky, or are they also cryptozoologists who hunt Bigfoot and the Mothman? Do they research alien abduction and read literature on ancient astronaut theory as well as study psi phenomena such as telekinesis? What, and, more importantly, *who* is the UFO subculture?

I want to be clear: this is not a book about UFOs. Rather, it is a book about the people who do not know what UFOs are, yet are attempting to piece the puzzle together. They are the *UFO subculture,* also referred to as the *UFO community,* and they are much more fascinating than the strange events and objects they hunt.

~

This book consists of two parts. Part 1 is a look at some individuals who make up the UFO subculture. It is a collection of stories, interviews and events, which represent the broader community. It is my personal experience with the process of researching and putting this book together. It highlights parts of my journey as I attempted to begin uncovering this curious culture. Furthermore, it highlights the fact that those who make up this subculture, more often than not, reside in a gap between worlds. On one hand, they wake up in the morning, they drink coffee, they drive their kids to school and dance class, they go to work, and function within "normal" (note the quotation marks) culture. On the other hand, they either have experienced or research things that challenge the very nature of "normal." They engage in the discourse of anomalous stuff—objects, entities and ideas which, according to a culture where everything is "normal," ought not to exist. Here, we take a brief look into the experiences of these individuals in an attempt to understand why the UFO phenomenon and its subculture are forced to exist upon the cultural edge.

Part 2 of this book is a theoretical treatise concerning the UFO community as a subcultural force. In other words, it hypothesizes and explores how the subculture affects and moves within broader mainstream culture. How does the UFO community interact with the rest of our collective culture, and how does it pose challenges and risks to our assumptions concerning how we go about our daily lives? In other words, how and why does the UFO community come to blows with "normal?" Part 2 will explore aspects of popular culture, science and the epistemology of the UFO experience, both as object and subject, in order to gain a better understanding of how the UFO community engages with itself and with those outside of it. I will conclude by calling into question the very nature of "normal," and argue that the very act of engaging with the UFO debate forces one to see beyond the illusion of the everyday. In more appropriate terms, what exactly do we mean by "alien" and does the UFO subculture alienate mainstream culture?

Both Part 1 and Part 2 of this book use a theoretical and philosophical foundation proposed by the late French philosopher Jacques Derrida. While I go into more detail concerning Derrida's philosophy later in the book, it presents, mainly, the UFO phenomenon and the UFO subculture as ghosts within our everyday society. My exploration of the UFO subculture led me to people who exist, or, rather, *haunt*, the broader mainstream cultural framework. The UFO community has dedicated much of their lives to the pursuit of the UFO, which is a phantom in and of itself. This strange phenomenon, this *ufological haunting*, has made the UFO community a ghost, and, in turn, establishes the spectrality of those who deem it possible to push them to the outside.

According to Derrida, ghosts, by their very nature, are both alive and dead, simultaneously real and imagined. UFOs and the UFO subculture are similar. They remind us that our everyday social world is in a similar state. Collectively, we measure ourselves *against the Other*, yet simultaneously, *we are that Other*. While this book will provide some speculative hypotheses as to the source of the UFO phenomenon, that is not its true focus. As I mentioned earlier, *I do not know*. Rather, this book will explore how these hypotheses influence and reshape the people who make up the UFO community. It will focus its lens upon the ideologies and paradigms, which give structure to the UFO narrative, and, by transitive property, the UFO community. We are, in essence, the stories we tell.

PART 1:

THE UFO PEOPLE

Oh me! Oh my!
Oh me! Oh my!
What a lot of funny things go by.
Some have two feet
And some have four.
Some have six feet
And some have more.
Where do they come from? I can't say.
But I bet they have come a long, long way.
We see them come.
We see them go.
Some are fast.
Some are slow.
Some are high
And some are low.
Not one of them
Is like another.
Don't ask us why.
Go ask your mother.

—DR. SEUSS,
FROM "ONE FISH, TWO FISH, RED FISH, BLUE FISH"

CHAPTER 1

A Cold Day in January

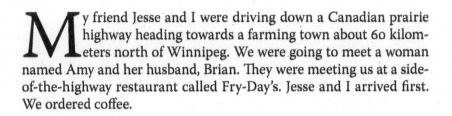

My friend Jesse and I were driving down a Canadian prairie highway heading towards a farming town about 60 kilometers north of Winnipeg. We were going to meet a woman named Amy and her husband, Brian. They were meeting us at a side-of-the-highway restaurant called Fry-Day's. Jesse and I arrived first. We ordered coffee.

Amy had filed a sighting report with the Mutual UFO Network, MUFON, and as I was the local field investigator, it was sent to me. I had joined MUFON roughly two years earlier. As a kid growing up, I was always fascinated by the strange and the weird. My parents would often watch shows like *The X-Files* or *The Outer Limits*, and, as an impressionable youngster, eerie ghosts and black eyed aliens became a part of my cable TV upbringing. We would often watch the various iterations of *Star Trek* and my parents kept quite a sizable library on three dark brown bookshelves in our basement. Much of it was science fiction or fantasy. It helped that most of my friends were geeks as well, and we would often have conversations about alien invasion or the existence of ghosts while riding our bikes around the neighbourhood.

In university, I was drawn to critical literary theory and culture studies. I was particularly interested in subcultures. Perhaps I like the underdog: those people who exist outside of the standards, which form *normal*. I am unsure why I find the study of subcultural groups interesting, but I continued my studies and became an educator. Many years later, through some mutual friends, I met a local UFO researcher and author named Chris Rutkowski. We became friends, and he decided that the best thing for me to do was to get involved in this "whole UFO thing." He informed me that there were a lot of stupid people out there, and that the UFO community, every once in a while, needed a "smart kid to stir the pot and piss a few people off." Chris not only showed me the door, he opened it for me. He then deliberately shoved me in.

I began to read books on the subject and started to participate in the various online UFO forums and social media platforms. I started my own blog a year later, and my aim was to explore the UFO issue from a more critical standpoint. I quickly realized I had no clue what the hell I was talking about. I had to get my hands dirty. I needed to investigate UFO reports.

I joined MUFON, bought the Field Investigator guide, passed the test, and, two weeks later, I was ready to start chasing UFOs. I imagined myself ripping down the highway on the tail of some fast-moving silver disc in my Toyota. The disc would disappear over some trees. I'd pull over to the side of the road, get out of the car, and, sure enough, through the thick brush, I would see the thing landed on the ground. I would approach slowly and cautiously, my brow soaked with sweat as I moved a leafy branch out of my way. Then suddenly, like a hunter, I'd crouch down and there they would be: three small gray aliens with huge black eyes, collecting samples of the local Canadian flora. I would silently reach into my top pocket and ever so slowly with great and significant caution, as to not attract their gaze, pull out my shiny brand new MUFON ID badge. I would then stumble out of the thicket towards them saying: "Hey! I'm with MUFON. What are you guys up to? Just collecting some samples? That's cool…"

Suffice it to say, my two-and-half years with MUFON was nothing like that. It was slow and tedious work at times. However, I quickly realized that the one thing I truly enjoyed was speaking to witnesses. There were no exciting UFO crashes to investigate, and certainly I did not bump into any alien beings, but I met people from all walks of life who were affected by one commonality: they saw something that made little sense, and that event shifted their perception of the world around them. Their experience, whatever it was, alienated them from their reality. They often felt like outcasts with respect to their old lives, and to the rest of the world. True underdogs. Outsiders.

I left MUFON shortly after I met Amy. However, I continued to investigate UFO sightings privately, and I continued to work with Amy after my role as MUFON Field Investigator came to an end.

My academic interest in subcultures seems to have embedded me, ironically, in the subculture that engages with the UFO phenomenon. I approached this entire ufological endeavour with no intention of becoming a part of the community, and yet it happened. I have definitely met some interesting people along the way, and that is fundamentally what this book is about. It is not about UFOs, not really. It is actually about people: people who do not fit. They are ghosts, in a sense, haunting the normal mainstream culture as well as the world of the paranormal; the fringes. The UFO subculture is a collection of outsiders, and this book will explore why.

Amy and Brian's farm was a little "out of the way" and did not show up on any maps that you could buy at a gas station, or even on Google Maps. Amy suggested that it would be simpler to meet at the diner and then follow them to their farm.

About five minutes after Jesse and I arrived, a couple walked into the restaurant. It was Amy who made eye contact with me. I smiled, and she gave a knowing nod. We made our introductions, chatted for a brief moment, and they headed out the door as I paid for the coffees. The server ringing up the cash register was a young woman, maybe twenty years old.

"Hey," I said, "that couple we were talking to. Do you know them?"

"They are in once in a while. Why?"

I looked over my shoulder at Amy and Brian getting into a large pick-up truck and Jesse leaning against the trunk of my car waiting to follow them to their farm on some remote country road. I chose my next words very carefully as I turned back to look at the server.

"They aren't axe murderers or anything, right?"

We left the diner's parking lot and drove for a few minutes down the highway. We then turned down a gravel provincial road, and eventually came upon an intersection of smaller gravel roads. Minutes later, we were at the farm. It was a beautiful prairie setting, and, even though it was winter and the fields were covered in two feet of snow, that sky rolled on into eternity. Jesse and I got out of the car. The couple walked over and welcomed us to their beautiful home.

We walked around the immediate grounds for about ten minutes as Amy went over the initial information regarding her sighting. She explained that she would always come out in the morning to feed and play with the barn cats. That particular morning, out of habit, she tossed one of the cats' toy balls into the sky. Looking up to catch it, she noticed something very peculiar—a silver round object, maybe a disc, hovering high above one of the barns, moving slowly towards the South. She guessed it was about 2000 feet in the air, like a low-flying aircraft, except this one made no noise, had no wings and looked like nothing she had ever seen. She remembers ducking down, crouching low, worried that it could come down at any moment. She reached into her coat pocket and snapped three pictures with her smartphone. The pictures showed nothing but an expansive sky and a curious blurry gray dot, far too mundane to be hard evidence. The object continued on a southward path for a minute or so until it disappeared over the barn roof and Amy lost sight of it. It simply disappeared.

Her sighting occurred in late September of 2016. Due to familial obligations, I was not able to meet with her until January of 2017, and a cold Canadian prairie wind had brought with it icy temperatures. We stood outside and looked up into the sky. Amy broke the short moment of silence by inviting us inside for coffee. The temperature was about -30 degrees Celsius and the sun was still low as it was early. Its bright warming light had little effect. Fortunately, it was a relatively still day. She suggested that we warm up and talk inside. I was glad. I forgot how much snow falls in the country compared with the city and realized that my shoes and my coat were not enough to keep me warm for long in this temperature. She and Brian began towards the house, while

Jesse and I stayed back for another moment. Jesse spoke first, looking up over the barn where Amy saw the curious object.

"What do you think?"

"Who knows. Could be anything."

We began walking to the house. "Interesting story," Jesse replied.

"Nothing I haven't heard before, but you never know."

I stopped and turned to look back at the barn. To say I looked back because I had an ominous feeling would be far too dramatic, but I felt compelled to. It was a niggling feeling in the back of my mind; a hunch that I ought to turn around and take one more look. I saw nothing but an empty sky. After taking in the scene, I turned and looked upon the massive open fields which, years ago, were grazing land for Brian's horses until he gave up farming but now sat covered in a blanket of white. It was a beautiful place: quiet and still. Suddenly, like a wild charging animal out of its hiding spot, a sharp, cold gust of wind came from across that open prairie field and slammed into me. It surprised me and nearly knocked me over. I became chilled very suddenly, and my thin coat did little to keep my body warm.

"Damn, it's cold!"

CHAPTER 2

Subcultures

Reflecting upon the very idea of UFOs compels a ridiculously simple assumption that is typically left out of ufological conversation: for UFOs to exist, people must exist. Whatever UFOs are, and whatever force, intelligence or construct causes them to be, hinges totally upon the human observer. Simply put, where there are people, there are UFOs. Author and researcher Chris Rutkowski publishes the annual Canadian UFO Survey, a yearly collection of categorized sighting reports across Canada and one of the few actual collections of its kind. When I asked Rutkowski about his statistics, he stated that "the UFO report numbers are correlated strongly with population." This is obvious. It makes sense. If no one is around to see a UFO, no one can report it. However, the more people who live in a given area, the more UFO reports there are from that area. It seems that UFOs, whatever they may be, follow and cluster around us. We are haunted by them. The question is, are they our collective ghosts who eerily whisper in our ears that we are not alone?

Without witnesses, without investigators, without the researchers and so-called "experts;" without ufologists and anyone else who partakes in UFO discourse, UFOs are merely objects, or things which can resemble objects. A thing cannot be *unidentified* if other things are not identified first, and identification requires human observation. In other words, I must know what a bird is before I can know what a bird is not. Furthermore, the very act of identification requires a paradigm from which to identify;

it requires a cultural place and an ideological framework. We create languages to communicate about things, ideas and values. We create letters and words, which represent "bird," for example. We also categorize, label, and dictate importance. We shape our beliefs and values around the identified things we deem important. You and I, our culture and environment, make UFOs real. That is not to say that we are delusional or make them up. We do, however, create for them a space within our frameworks from which they can remain *unidentified*.

For some, UFOs are merely the product of fantasy and not worthy of serious time or consideration. They are a product of delusion and best served up as comedic relief. This position is held strongly by mainstream media, for example. For others, they are very real and of incredible importance. They drive a desire to come face-to-face with a strange unknowable thing. The people who are driven to the UFO question form a subculture, and they shape the reality of the UFO phenomenon.

A subculture is "a group of people who consciously define themselves as different or apart from the culture to which they officially belong."[2] Dick Hebdige, the foremost theorist on subcultures, argued that, by definition, a subculture must form what he refers to as *style*. In his book, *Subculture: Meaning of Style*, he writes that a subculture is "a form of resistance in which experienced contradictions and objections to [a] ruling ideology are obliquely represented in style.[3]

Hebdige's work primarily focused on British subcultures, such as the punk music scene, in the late seventies and eighties. Other theorists have since expanded upon his concept of *style*, since not all subcultures have a "physical" style, but rather share a common identity. Ken Gelder, author of *Subcultures: Cultural Histories and Social Practice*, writes that "the most common narrative about subcultures is, of course, one that casts them as nonconformist and non-normative: different, dissenting, or...'deviant.'"[4]

As Gelder explains, a subculture is "alienated"[5] from the mainstream or popular culture. It is "pitched against the conformist pressures

---

[2] Buchanan, Ian. Oxford Dictionary of Critical Theory. Oxford University Press: New York. 2010.

[3] Hebdige, Dick. Subculture: Meaning of Style. Routledge New York 1979, 133.

[4] Gelder, Ken. Subcultures; Cultural Histories and Social Practice. Routledge: New York. 2007, 3.

[5] Ibid, 4.

of mass society" and often works, both openly and/or unknowingly against those pressures.

Finally, and perhaps most importantly, Gelder points out that a subculture:

> carries a set of narratives about itself, some of which are generated internally while others, usually more visible and pervasive, are developed and deployed in and by the society around it... Narratives by or about a subculture come into being and produce a set of effects (or, affects) and reactions: fascination, envy, anxiety, disdain, revulsion, legislation, social reform, etc. They are never neutral. Every narrative by or about a subculture is a matter of position-taking – both within that subculture and outside it.[6]

A subculture is a group of people with a common narrative, one that they create themselves, and one that is created by those outside of that culture about them. Those narratives, those stories, push that subculture into a cultural and social place from which it often differentiates and deviates from the mainstream and the popular. When it comes to the people who participate in the UFO discourse, often referred to as the UFO community or the UFO subculture, one can only hope there is appreciation for the irony of being *alienated* by the rest of society.

Much work has been done in an attempt to understand how the UFO subculture functions, but it has generally been a relatively simplistic approach. Folklorist Dr. David Clarke suggests that there are three groups that form the main body of the UFO subculture. They are: The General Public, Ufologists, and Experiencers.[7] He breaks these groups down as follows:

The general public has a relatively limited knowledge base concerning the UFO phenomenon. Their understanding generally concerns the mainstream or popular paradigms concerning the UFO phenomenon. A person in this group may have seen a documentary or two, films on the subject, or read a book or article. In simple terms, they have a general understanding of what a UFO is, but that is all. Clarke writes that

---

[6]   Ibid, 2.

[7]   Clarke, David. "Extraordinary Experiences with UFOs." *The Ashgate Research Companion to Paranormal Cultures*. Routledge. 2014, 90.

the beliefs of this group are not particularly "consistent or coherent"[8] as they possess limited knowledge. Much of their knowledge is sourced from concepts presented on *The X-Files*, The History Channel's *Ancient Aliens*, or other popular media.

Ufologists form the next level of the subculture. They have increased knowledge concerning the UFO phenomenon, and typically form groups to actively study, investigate and research UFO events. They range from critical skeptics to overzealous believers, and often debates rage on between members of this group concerning the validity of evidence, cases, and data. To put it bluntly, the advent of the Internet and social media has generated significant chaos amongst this group. More on this later.

This ufologist group, according to author Bryan Appleyard, is divided into three main ideological belief systems. There are those who believe UFOs are "nuts and bolts" alien spacecraft, physical and technological, from a distant planet. The next group are those who believe, in what Appleyard calls, the "Third Realm" which is essentially a more mystical interpretation of the phenomenon, such as interdimensional or supernatural beings where physicality and objectivity ranges, depending upon the individual's interpretation. One interpretation, which will be presented later in this book, the realm of the *Mundus Imaginalis* as postulated by philosopher Henry Corbin, will be presented. The third segment consists of those who believe in the psychosocial hypothesis, that is, the UFO is a product of the mind or the collective unconscious, most famously posited by Carl Jung.[9] The key point, which Clarke and Appleyard do not address, is that these systems often intermix, and the divisions between these paradigms are not rigid at all. Many individuals within the community borrow various aspects from all three segments to form a hypothesis or theory.

Lastly, Clarke asserts that those who have directly been contacted or abducted by aliens form the final level of the community. These community members have experienced some sort of life-altering event that has galvanized their fundamental conviction for the UFO phenomenon. Beyond that, it has become a part of their life. Some choose to cease engagement with the phenomenon and prefer to avoid it totally. Some choose to form support groups for others who have experienced similar events, and some even go so far as to create religions and cults, a few of

---

[8] Ibid.

[9] Appleyard, Bryan. *Aliens: Why They Are Here*. Scribner Press. 2005

which have ended in tragedy such as the Heaven's Gate suicide in 1997, in which they promote the messages given to them by "the beings."[10]

Clarke and Appleyard provide a good overview of the community, and, upon first glance, their interpretation seems to paint a picture of the subculture. However, they do not dig deep enough into the anarchic ideologies of the subculture itself. Furthermore, the relationships and ideologies of individuals within the groups are much more nuanced than what Clarke and Appleyard present. Many of these groups inter-mix, shift and adjust almost constantly. Members within those groups will sometimes "excommunicate" each other, or at least attempt to, and often question each other's intentions, honesty, loyalty and research. In simple terms, there is little agreement from within as to who forms the community. Are all the groups mentioned above the UFO subcul-ture, or only certain segments? Herein lies a fundamental question.

Clarke and Appleyard oversimplify a very complex collection of people; a group, which does not lend itself well to categorization and grouping, as this book will attempt to prove. No one really knows where they stand within the subculture, as the foundation of the subculture, its place within history and mythology, is, oddly enough, totally alien.

Cultural theorist Jodi Dean states that the UFO community is, "an-yone with a strong interest in UFOs..." However, she points out that the term gets "fuzzy around the edges and not everyone agrees who's in and who's out." She addresses the fact that many people who have seen UFOs or had other related experiences never become involved in the discourse and choose to move on from their experience simply by trying to forget about it. They distance themselves from the UFO community as much possible. That being said, many who do have cu-rious ufological experiences do begin to engage in the conversation. Dean cuts her definition of the UFO community down to one simple idea: "people in the UFO community have a general sense of what the term means."[11] Simply put, members of the community just know if they belong or not.

As Dean suggests, it is impossible to delineate subcultural borders for this community. While people within the UFO subculture gener-ally understand what the term "*UFO community*" means, there is little awareness of how the subculture looks or operates. One cannot frame it,

---

[10]   Clarke, 91

[11]   Dean. Jodi. *Aliens in America.* Cornell University Press. New York. 1998, 18.

nor provide an exact definition of who is a member, and who is not. Its membership is fluid, and, most importantly of all, it defies and reframes our very definitions of *subculture*. However, we can explore the historical events, mythologies, and ideologies that form the UFO discourse, and, in turn, gain insight into the people who engage with that discourse.

Diving into this historical and mythological realm of the UFO subculture requires addressing a fundamental aspect of UFO discourse. Regardless of one's beliefs regarding the UFO phenomenon, of which there are many, the UFO community is permanently tied to the construct of the alien visitor—the *extraterrestrial*. The alien has become mythologized. Its place within popular culture, and within the interior of the UFO subculture itself, has fundamentally shifted the way society and the world is interpreted—a sort of physical boundary for *the Other*. Even more fascinating is how the extraterrestrial has affected the framework of the UFO subculture and created a community of people who fundamentally challenge the status quo.

As mentioned previously, narratives are what generate the identity of a subculture. To begin to understand the UFO community, we must attempt to understand the tales they tell, and the tales that are told about them. This collection of narratives comes together to form common sets of ideological paradigms, mythologies, tenets, knowledge and beliefs. These concepts form inside and around the subculture, and shape how members of the community interact with each other, with the discourse, and with mainstream culture. Perception of the community from within and from without establishes the reality of that community. However, what happens when a subculture does not obey this principle? What occurs when a subculture is not merely deviant, as Gelder argues all must be, but instead disregards the very reality, which forms mainstream culture?

This book will present the UFO subculture from the standpoint of the *Other* because the subculture approaches contemporary social paradigms in this way. The UFO community does not fit the traditional understanding of subculture because it does not function in strictly "human" terms. That is not to say that extraterrestrials or non-human entities are real. Rather, the very existence of the UFO subculture challenges the validity of the cultural reality that we take for granted. The UFO community is the alien, and it also alienates the ideologies and consensus that the vast majority of us have agreed to.

We must begin to chisel away a foothold to better understand this subculture, and, in turn, glean insight into a community of people who not only challenge normalized mainstream culture, but also punch through the very fabric of normal itself. Studying UFOs is all well and good. However, to truly begin to understand them as objects and as subjects, we must attempt to shape our understanding of the people who regularly engage with them in various ways. In no uncertain terms, without people, there are no UFOs.

First, this book will present several individuals who are engaged with the UFO phenomenon in some way, and the discourse, which surrounds the phenomenon. Amy, whom I have already mentioned, and the others in this book, will provide an experiential foundation. Through their experiences, research and work, I hope to enrich the general understanding of the UFO phenomenon and the community. Further, they will serve as examples for the broader picture I wish to paint. I hope to present an original interpretation and framework for the UFO subculture based upon the work of French philosopher Jacques Derrida. Using his notion and conceptualization of *the ghost*, which will be described later, I wish to present the UFO community as something real and not real. The UFO community exists, in that it functions like any other subculture, albeit chaotically; yet by its very existence, it flips mainstream culture upon its head and severs all ties between what we deem to be real and not real. It is a subculture, yet it is not because it asserts that there is no *culture to be a substratum of.* Derrida's ghosts exist in a dualistic realm, simultaneously present in our world yet not there at all. We, as a culture, are haunted by the phenomenon itself; moreover, we are also haunted by the people who shape that phenomenon.

CHAPTER 3

Haunted Manitoba

Amy and Brian turned out to be the kindest people I had ever met. Brian, a strong but quiet man who is old enough to be retired but is too hardworking to stop, had never even thought about UFOs until his wife claimed to have witnessed one. Brian, a successful and sought-after mechanical engineer, is a no-nonsense guy. He would give you the shirt off his back before you even had to ask, and while a UFO would have been something he would probably have laughed off, if his wife says she saw one, she damn well saw one.

Amy is a retired flight attendant turned writer. Living on a quiet farm where the solitude allowed her to draft her first novel. Clever, creative and funny, she found the whole UFO thing rather silly until one calm quiet evening she looked out her bedroom window and saw something she could not explain.

The town of Teulon in Manitoba, Canada, sits between two large lakes—Lake Manitoba to the west and Lake Winnipeg to the East. The land that runs between these two lakes, wherein Teulon is situated, is predominantly farm land. To this day, even centuries after colonization, much of this land remains covered in thick patches of forest. It is a strange mix of peaceful farm land, with wide open stretches of canola and wheat, and dense forests and untouched provincial park land that takes up innumerable acres.

Roughly 60 kilometers South is the provincial capital of Winnipeg, with a population nearing a million people, and a couple of hundred kilometers more, the border which separates Canada from North Dakota, and the United States. To the North, a dozen or so other small farming towns populate the wide expanses of prairie. The land, before the arrival of Europeans, was predominantly home to the Cree, Ojibway, Dene and the Dakota. While other indigenous groups also used the land between and around the two lakes, several reservations also occupy this area.

Boundary lines run along this whole area and separate land which belongs to the province and the reservation land which dots the coasts of the two lakes and farther on into the more Northern reaches of Manitoba. Amy and Brian's farm sits a few kilometers from the town of Teulon itself, and, for their privacy, its exact location will remain unpublished.

Amy recounted several of her experiences, which will be presented in the upcoming chapters, but I wish to jump ahead for a moment in this story. I discovered that the area has had quite a few sightings of strange lights in the sky and anomalous encounters with bizarre craft. There are rumours that large subterranean rivers run under the earth connecting the two lakes. Many small towns dot the area, and it is also believed that deep limestone caverns sit well beneath the layers of soil that lend themselves so well to farming.

~

Roughly forty kilometers north of Teulon sits Narcisse, a large snake den which houses tens of thousands of garter snakes. The snakes, during the winter, live in a massive network of underground limestone caverns. In the spring and summer, the snakes migrate out of these caverns to mate, and the Narcisse area becomes overrun by the creatures and by thousands of tourists who come to see this migration. Several farmers in and around the Teulon area, and other nearby farming towns, have reported massive numbers of garter snakes pouring out of the ground on their property. They believe that there are massive limestone tunnels which run all around Manitoba, and, at times, the snakes make their way through this underground maze. Some ufologists have suggested that limestone, for some reason, attracts UFOs and other paranormal phenomena. Obviously, the evidence for such a claim is non-existent beyond a possible correlation between sightings and the bedrock beneath the surface of a given area.

One other curious story is that Lake Winnipeg itself acts as a sort of beacon or portal for paranormal activity. For many local indigenous groups, the lake is not only important for resources but for spiritual reasons as well. Many eyewitness reports have been made concerning strange lights hovering over the lake, descending into and emerging from the waters. There has even been a fair share of monster sightings, some in the water and some in the dense wilderness, which surrounds much of the expansive coastline. One such creature, which connects to indigenous Ojibway and Cree mythology, is the Wendigo.

While the legend has variations, the local area seems to hold a very consistent lore concerning the Wendigo. It is, in simple terms, a spirit that is able to possess a human. The Wendigo will often seek out someone who is alone, typically in the wilderness or via a dream, and drive them mad. The victim often develops a blood lust, experiences psychotic rage, and has the desire to consume human flesh. While many of my colleagues in the Southern United States will often compare the Wendigo to the Navajo legend of the Skinwalker, there are some key differences; the main one being that the Skinwalker is more akin to a witch or shaman who has made a deal with an evil spirit and become powerful albeit corrupted by the compact. The Wendigo itself is a spirit. Secondly, a person is usually possessed by the Wendigo spirit, and does not seek one to commune with. Lastly, when the Wendigo does possess a human host, they will not transform or shape-shift.

However, the legend does go deeper beyond a demon like spirit able to possess hapless victims. The Wendigo spirit itself can physically manifest, and it usually does for its intended target. While the appearance varies based upon tribal group, it is typically 8 or 9 feet tall with a human-like appearance. It is gaunt, thin, and resembles a rotting corpse; it even gives off the smell of decay and death. Many interpretations of the legend have also suggested that it possess deer-like antlers; however, I'm convinced that this is a modern addition to the story.

The vast majority of reports concerning the Wendigo involve possession. When local authorities are sent to investigate a homicide, it has been claimed by witnesses, on rare occasions, that the killer was possessed by the spirit. One report, made in the early 1900s, involved a local community's being forced to kill a man because he went on a rampage, killing most of his family and even a neighbour. The local elders, in their report to the authorities, claimed that the man was possessed by a Wendigo. Physical manifestations of the spirit are very rare, as any person who sees a Wendigo usually does not make it out of the situation alive. Usually. I have heard stories from people who claim to have seen the monster.

One particular story told to me involved a man driving down a highway towards his home in a small town on the southern edge of Lake

Winnipeg late at night when he saw something dark hunched over on the side of the road. Thinking it was someone in distress, he slowed down and flashed his high beams on to get a better look. Just as he was nearing what he thought was a man, the figure turned to face the car, and rose to what the witness could only guess to be eight feet in height. With long gangly limbs, large claw like hands, and eyes, which seemed to be either black or simply empty sockets, the creature quickly dashed towards the car. The man swerved into the oncoming lane, which, fortunately, was empty due to the late hour, and accelerated quickly. He lost sight of the thing, but, afraid that it was trying to chase him down, he maintained a high rate of speed, about 140 kilometers per hour on the highway, and went straight home. He admitted to being afraid and chose not to leave his home for several days. He even kept his hunting rifle loaded by his bed for the next two weeks. Perhaps he fell asleep at the wheel for a brief moment and dreamed the whole thing up, or the local legends, which have been on the lips of the local indigenous groups, and indigenous groups across Canada for thousands of years, are true. Many of the local communities, however, remain tight-lipped concerning their Wendigo stories. Similar to the Navajo Skinwalker legend, speaking of the creature will bring about bad luck, or even worse, a visit from the creature itself.

The area is also home to many UFO sightings. There's a significant number of stories from the Teulon area, as well as the surrounding towns, but, for the purpose of this book, I will provide only a few examples. This is in no way an exhaustive list, and significant research into the local UFO and paranormal stories has already been done by Manitoba author and researcher Chris Rutkowski. My intention, here, is to lend some evidence to the fact that people in the area, apart from Amy, are witnessing, or at least talking about witnessing, strange objects in the sky.

One such individual, an older gentleman with whom I spoke on the telephone, told me a story from when he was a young boy, about 5 or 6 years old, in 1955 or 1956. He remembered lying on the couch, and he seemed to recall it was sometime in the morning, when he heard his mother in the kitchen gasp and yell for his father. He ran to the kitchen and he was told to stay inside the house. He recalled his mother and father running outside of their small farmhouse and darting towards the back field. Seeing that his older sisters had no intention of missing out on the fun, he too decided to disregard his parents' instructions and followed them outside. Turning the corner of the house, he remembers freezing in his tracks and almost bumping into his father's behind: around 50 meters away, a large silver-metallic disc was resting in the middle of their wheat field. His parents, his sisters and he stood there for a minute or so, dumbfounded. The object then slowly and silently rose off the ground and took off straight up into the sky.

The look on their father's face was a mix of fear and deep concentration, and the witness explained that he and his sisters knew that one word out of their mouths at that time would warrant a stern look and some "country discipline." He recalled that no one spoke about what happened until that evening. The family ate their dinner in silence until his father, putting down his cutlery with some force, looked at his mother and said, "it's those damn Russians."

His last memory regarding the sighting was from the next day when his uncle, his father's brother, came by the farm to hear the story. The witness explained that no one else was told about this event. Being *that* family in such a close-knit farming community would label you permanently, and his father was not willing to take the risk. The last thing they wanted was to have rumours spread about their being crazy. He remembered seeing the large impression where the object had sat on the ground. The wheat crushed down and flattened in a circle, which he guessed to be about twenty feet in diameter.

When I asked him if I could visit the farm where this happened, he explained that it was sold in the seventies to another family. He explained that after the harvest and the next year's planting, the land grew the crop without any problems.

Interestingly, Teulon had another alleged UFO landing in December of 1978 when an anonymous report was made concerning a green fireball that lit up the sky over a farm. Similar to the previous story, the green fireball came down in a field and left a sizeable hole in the ground. Unfortunately, this incident and the previous one cannot be confirmed by any means.

I was informed of another case, this time by fellow author Chris Rutkowski, which took place in late March of 1980. In his book, *Unnatural History: True Manitoba Mysteries*, he presents the case of a man who was recovering in Teulon's hospital. A little after midnight, the man looked out his window and saw an approximately thirty-foot-long football shaped object hovering over a nearby building. Dotted with multi-coloured Christmas style lights, the object moved in a southeasterly direction, passing near the hospital window where the man was standing. Suddenly, multiple lights turned on around the middle of the craft, illuminating what appeared to be the interior of the craft. The man witnessed four individuals inside who looked human with very short hair styles. The interior lights went out, and the object then moved away into the distance. It then turned and moved towards the west. A short time later, the same object then turned around and moved towards the east, out of the man's view. The man called for a nurse, and, upon her arrival, he explained the situation and asked that she remain to also see the object. It never returned.

In more recent years, a case from June 1999 describes a husband and wife driving home down the highway at 11:00 PM. The couple reported the case to PSICAN (Paranormal Studies and Inquiry Canada). A bright white globe-shaped light hovered roughly five feet above their vehicle as they were traveling down the highway away from Teulon and south towards Winnipeg. The wife, in the passenger seat, saw it first through the windshield. She alerted her husband who looked up and also saw the light. It was totally silent and solid in colour, without blinking or variation. It was very bright, but he noted that it did not hurt the eyes. He looked down at the road, and then back up at the light, but it vanished.

Jesse and I sat in Amy's living room in a lovely home; warm, and a stark contrast to the bleak winter outside its walls. I asked her to tell us her story. She began by explaining that her sighting in September was not her first, nor her most recent. She explained that her first sighting occurred in 2012, and, since being in contact with me, she had witnessed additional strange objects in the sky above her farm. She had also experienced the sighting of what she could only describe as a ghost. Perhaps two or three minutes had passed, and, in that time, three thoughts were simultaneously running through my mind. Amy was hallucinating, making all this up, or, the worst-case scenario, whatever the phenomenon was, it was haunting her like some specter. The following is her story.

Late in the evening in mid-June of 2012, Amy was watching television in her bedroom. The world outside her window was dark and empty with the only light being the stars in the night sky. The window faced out onto the fields of the farm, which roll on and on into the distant prairie horizon. While she was watching her television program, a warm sensation came over her: what she describes as a "thin veil of warm water." Feeling compelled to look out the window, she witnessed a massive object. From what Amy could see, it had an oblong shape, like a cigar, with long thin bars protruding all around it, and the bottom of it hovered about 90 meters from her window over the yard. The size of the object was immense, like a shopping mall or several city-blocks in size. It climbed high into the sky for several hundred meters, and Amy was unable visually to take in the entire object. It was glowing orange. Amy describes the colour as being "the colour of hot ash when a bonfire gets low."

She recalls sitting there, motionless, as if she was prey studying a predator, knowing full well that the predator was studying her as well. She felt as if she was being observed, read like a book, and that, whatever it was, it was presenting itself to her.

Its hold on her lasted only a few moments. She eventually leapt out of bed and pressed herself up against the window pane trying to get a better look. It was gone. It did not fly into the distance or higher into the sky; it simply disappeared. I conclude with Amy's own words:

> I didn't know what to make of it. What was it that I saw? I wanted to be invisible to this thing but how was that possible now? This thing knows of me, where to find me, when to find me. It had touched me. I had touched it, even with just my eyes. It altered a mortal being, me, because that is distinctly what occurred. I was altered in some way and have never been the same since.

The next several years for Amy were dotted with odd events. However, similar to a compulsion, Amy looks out that window every night before she goes to bed, even to this day. I want to point out that when I met Amy and investigated her sightings, all I had was testimony (and that's all I have today). Many airplanes fly through the skies above her farm, but her past working in close proximity to various aircraft would rule out an inability to identify a conventional aircraft. Furthermore, I have been unable to find any evidence of aircraft being in the air during the times she has seen these objects. No flights are logged during the moments of her sightings. Does this rule out conventional and prosaic explanations? No. There is no physical evidence to support her encounters with UFOs. I cannot prove her story, but I cannot disprove it. I simply do not know. I have no idea what Amy saw in 2016 or in 2012, but, whatever it was, it has clearly affected her. As I reiterate often in this book and in my other work, the UFO as object is fundamentally less important than *the interpretation and the individual who experienced the phenomenon.* Still, even without tangible proof, I have no reason to doubt Amy's story.

The more she attempted to find answers, the more often curious events would occur. Whatever the phenomenon is, it seems to haunt both the people who engage with it and the very underpinnings of a municipal community. The very act of my coming into contact with Amy has created a small buzz amongst certain people in the town. In quiet conversations over coffee, people speak not about the weather or the latest movie they saw at the cinema, but of UFOs and their encounters with them. Certain looks are exchanged, and the conversation ceases when the server comes by to refill the cup. The air seems different, not because the phenomenon is present, but because people are speaking of it. Their communication is bringing something to life, a feeling or emotion or construct from some unknown state, and, in turn, altering the very fabric of their reality.

My friend Jesse, who traveled with me to Amy's property, also experienced a UFO sighting a year after meeting Amy. Whether Amy's sightings and Jesse's sighting are connected, I do not know. However, for the sake of posterity, here is his story.

About 45 kilometers northeast of Amy's property is the small fishing town of Gimli, Manitoba. It sits on the western coast of Lake Winnipeg and is an idyllic little place. With a population around 2,500 people, the town economically relies on fishing, the local rye whiskey distillery, and on tourism in the summer when it becomes filled with cottagers and visitors to its beaches. The town was founded in 1875 by Icelandic settlers due to a series of volcanic eruptions in Iceland that forced a small group to relocate. By the 1930s, the town was a booming tourist spot and remains so today. By their own admission, the town's residents, many of which are descendants of the Icelanders who arrived over a century ago, are very superstitious by nature. The town is home to a public park with tiny little homes for Iceland's various legendary supernatural creatures, such as elves and the Huldufólk, or hidden people. Gimli also plays host to many tales of strange creatures: Sasquatch, lake monsters, ghosts and UFO sightings over the town and the lake. Jesse grew up in Gimli, and his parents' residence is a little north of the town. While Jesse lives in Winnipeg, he and his girlfriend were visiting his mom and dad for Christmas.

Jesse and his girlfriend were returning to bed after getting a couple of glasses of water in the early morning of Christmas Day in 2017. It was approximately 4:30am when they returned to their bedroom. Being roughly 12 kilometers north of Gimli, the sky was clear of any light pollution and clouds. The stars shone brightly as the two returned to bed. Jesse gazed out the window for several minutes, and, just as he was about to return to sleep, he noticed something strange to the west.

A single flashing orb-like object dropped quickly through the sky on a vertical trajectory. Jesse guesses it was roughly 10–15 thousand feet up, and simply appeared and began to fall straight down. It cycled through several colours, but Jesse recalls that red seemed to be the main hue of the object, followed by yellow and white as being the second most common. It fell quickly for about four seconds before it came to a sudden stop. It then proceeded to quickly bounce around the sky. Jesse likened the erratic movements to that of a ping pong ball being pelted around. Performing this chaotic routine for several seconds, the object then turned white and proceeded quickly south along a horizontal flight path. After about ten seconds, the object disappeared out of eyeshot into the distant southern sky. Jesse describes the horizontal movement as being like a fish swimming through water and guesses that it had been traveling around 300 kilometers per hour.

Jesse and his girlfriend both saw the object, and he admits to having no clue what it was. Jesse in particular felt that this object was engaged in some sort of performance and that it was aware of them as observers. He admits that this sounds cliché, but he also cannot shake the curious feeling that the object left him with. Moments before he was going to close his eyes, the object appeared suddenly. Jesse cannot point to any clear indicator that this object appeared specifically for him, but, much like the gut feeling that you get that when you feel as if you are being watched, he cannot shake the hunch.

Similar to Amy with her encounters, and countless other UFO witnesses in the reams of ufological literature, Jesse had, what can only be described as, "a feeling." Indeed, this could all simply be coincidence or a product of human psychology. Or, as others argue, such as author and researcher Dr. Dean Radin, humans have a sixth sense which somehow is able to perceive data and information that is not always accessible by the main five senses.

Thousands of small towns across the globe can offer up similar tales of anomalous encounters with strange lights and even the occasional monster and cryptid. Millions of people also make similar claims. Amy, and her town Teulon, and Jesse and the often-haunted town of Gimli, do not stand out as some curious outliers. These bizarre events and hidden conversations are not unique. Amy's experiences are not unique. All towns and many people within them can undoubtedly boast similar stories, and this should give one pause. This phenomenon is ubiquitous. It is present because people report it, and absent because the understanding among the general mainstream public is that UFOs and aliens are not real. As objects, UFOs are there and then suddenly not. The phenomenon seems to be everywhere, in every small town, haunting people, and impossible to pin down; a ghost.

CHAPTER 4

The Woman on the Porch

S even months before Amy's initial UFO sighting, she encountered what she could only describe as a ghost. Many UFO researchers and writers have argued that UFO events, ghosts and other paranormal phenomena seem to go hand in hand. In their book, *Hunt for the Skinwalker*, Dr. Colm Kelleher and George Knapp explore the possibility that many UFO events are somehow connected to various other paranormal and supernatural events. Poltergeist activity, sightings of Bigfoot, and strange lights in the sky seem to permeate our world and are often seen together or within close proximity. If Kelleher and Knapp are correct, then the UFO phenomenon is not entirely an alien one, comprising flesh and blood extraterrestrials, but of something much more strange and bizarre. In his book *The Mothman Prophecies*, John Keel makes similar claims. The monsters, aliens and UFOs that occupy both our physical world and our minds may be connected in some way.

This begs an interesting question: is this phenomenon an intelligent Other, or is it a reflection of us—of our dreams and anxieties? Or, even more compelling, is it both? Amy, who, since 2012, has witnessed multiple strange objects above her farm, does not have an answer. However, on one sunny Fall day in 2011, Amy had her first encounter with something that escaped from some unknown gap between worlds.

It was warm that day, Amy recalls. The sun was shining, and she was happy to be outside. Her neighbour, Jane (pseudonym), who lived a five-minute walk up the road, was away traveling. She and her family headed south to the United States for some much-needed holiday time. Jane had a relative, a young woman, house-sitting while they were away. She was a student and was often away during the day attending classes or working. Jane also had several dogs, and, during the times when her house-sitter was away, they were locked up in the garage. Amy knew the dogs well and was told that she could walk them whenever she would like. Noting how lovely the day was, Amy decided that she would let the cooped-up animals out for some air. She began to walk up the road towards her neighbour's house.

The road was quiet and secluded. There were no cars to disturb the peaceful walk to the neighbour's farm. Amy eventually reached the long lane which led up to her neighbour's property. Amy was feeling happy, elated even, at the thought of being with the dogs. They were well-tempered farm animals, and nothing would make them happier than running around the wide-open field and going for a walk up the country road. As Amy made her way up the long lane to the house, she noticed someone inside the screened porch. A woman was sitting in a chair, watching Amy come up the lane. As Amy got closer, she noticed the woman's cold emotionless stare. Amy smiled as she approached the porch, but the woman's face remained unchanged. It was an uncaring scowl, and Amy felt that the woman wanted nothing to do with her. Amy was an unwanted visitor. It was then that Amy noticed the woman was holding a coffee mug in her left hand, her arm slightly raised as if she was about to take her next sip, or at least pondering it.

At first, Amy thought that this was Jane's young house sitter but quickly realized that this woman was much too old. She had blonde hair, wore brightly patterned glasses, and looked to be in her early sixties. Amy immediately knew that this woman did not want her there. A feeling of discomfort came over Amy. She glanced away, unable to take the woman's gaze. When Amy looked back, the woman had risen from her chair in the corner and walked towards the door that led to the kitchen. She disappeared into the shadows of the porch and Amy lost sight of her. Amy, feeling uncomfortable, began to walk towards the garage. It was then that she realized the dogs were silent. No barking. No movement whatsoever.

Amy opened the door to let the dogs out, and the silent animals simply looked at her, quietly. On every other occasion, the dogs would have bounded out with delight in their usual frisky manner. She leashed them and took them down the lane towards the country road for their walk. After a few minutes of walking, Amy felt the need to tell her husband about this strange woman inside her neighbour's house. Using her mobile phone, she called Brian asking if he knew of anyone else staying in Jane's home, and she informed him of this woman's strange behaviour. Brian told her, "It's probably just another relative. Just leave her alone. Sometimes people are just odd."

Amy felt that something was wrong. She cut the walk short and took the dogs back home. She decided to play with them in the yard, and the dogs were happy to run about chasing a thrown stick. She noticed, at one point, that their water bowl was empty. Staring at the bowl, she suddenly realized she had to go inside the house. That feeling of discomfort returned. She did not want to disturb the woman who clearly did not want her there. Picking up the bowl, she unlocked the back door and went into the kitchen. Calling out to let the home's occupant know that she was there, she yelled, "It's just me. Just filling the water bowl..." She filled the bowl and left as quickly as possible.

Returning to the dogs, she placed the bowl down and continued to play with them. Suddenly, a feeling of nausea came over her. She was going to be sick. Fighting off the urge to throw up, Amy knew she had to go home. She began to corral the dogs back into the garage, but they had little interest in returning. They disobeyed her. She allowed them to play for a few more minutes, but the feeling became unbearable. She had to leave. It took much cajoling, but the dogs eventually returned, albeit reluctantly, to the garage. She began to make her way around the house. Although feeling very unwell, she felt the urge to peer into the porch through one of the screen windows. The woman was not there, but, when Amy saw the door that led into the kitchen, the same door that the woman had used to walk into the house, Amy realized she had just seen something impossible. Large boxes were piled high in front of the door. Her neighbour, Jane, had been using the screened porch as temporary storage. The door was blocked, and it would take quite some time to move all the boxes out of the way. Amy left quickly. Something was terribly wrong.

Jane and her family eventually returned home from their vacation. Jane, wanting to thank Amy, invited her over for a glass of wine. Amy was afraid to set foot in that house but knew that Jane needed to know about what happened. Amy asked if anyone else was staying the house besides her niece. Jane, confused by the question, said "No." Wondering why Amy looked so puzzled, Jane asked her to explain.

Amy recounted the story about the older blonde woman with the glasses, cold and unfriendly, sitting in the corner of the screened in porch, with a coffee mug in her hand. Jane became quiet. The entire house, Amy recalls, shifted into complete and utter silence. Jane looked at her friend and asked, "Would you know the person if I showed you a picture?"

Amy assured her she would, and Jane showed Amy a framed photograph on a shelf. Amy looked at the two women in the photo, and she felt suddenly comforted. Yes! There she was. Amy pointed to the woman on the right, informing Jane that she was here. Relief came over Amy. It wasn't some stranger, but someone Jane knew.

Jane's face paled and then she burst into tears. The woman in the photograph was Jane's mother who died in April, only months before Amy saw her in the screened-in porch. In her sixties, she was diagnosed with cancer. Jane's mother, when she was alive, would often sit in the chair in the corner of the porch, drinking cup after cup of coffee. Amy recounted a joke Jane told her about her mother: she "had more coffee in her bloodstream than blood."

Amy comforted her friend, but, in the back of her mind, she realized that she had just witnessed something impossible, something that should not be. There was no going back now. The world made a little less sense. Whatever it was: a spirit, a specter, or a phantasmal representation of some deep latent ability within Amy, a myth made real, this ghost opened Amy to the phenomenon. Whatever doorway it was guarding, it unlocked the door for Amy. It showed her that something was on the other side, something unknown, and perhaps, in its own way, dared her to step through. Once that door opened, however, everything on that side would also be able to come to this side.

CHAPTER 5

Gender Politics and Flying Saucers

~

I wish temporarily to leave Amy's story here. We will return to it. However, during my series of meetings, phone calls, e-mails and visits with Amy, something else was brewing... my coffee.

I was sitting in a coffee shop—a place called Thom Bargen Coffee. The clicking of laptop keyboards hummed in the background like a thousand mechanical crickets. It was a popular hangout for bloggers, university students, and writers because the WiFi was free, they had a long table with plugs that ran along the middle for charging, and the coffee was good. The guys sporting beards and man-buns behind the counter added the hipster flare, and plaid seemed to be the uniform of choice. I ordered my coffee, sat down, and opened up my laptop. I scrolled through the various emails, messages and tweets concerning the latest in ufology. I was drawn to a tweet from blogger Mike Damante, author of *Punk Rock and UFOs*, and his interview with UFO researcher and radio host Erica Lukes. Clicking the link, I went to his blog.

I was drawn to a quote from Lukes:

> Being a female researcher in a male-dominated field has its challenges, and one of them is dealing with the overt sexism that runs rampant in the field. Unfortunately, there are organizations, "researchers" and prominent members of the community who turn a blind eye to this

type of behavior when they should be addressing the issue and taking the lead on mandating professional and ethical standards. We often complain about the fact that we are not taken seriously and when we engage in unprofessional behavior, we demean the hard work of many who have come before us.[12]

Lukes continued:

It is vital to bring more *women* and a younger generation into the field. The younger generation is savvy enough to understand examples of sexism and racism and they will even speak out about it. When women are demeaned and even "slut shamed," we have a serious problem and it becomes time to shine a spotlight on the people who engage in this abuse, so we can clean up the field and get back to quality research.[13]

I had never considered the inherent problems that exist with gender in the UFO subculture. I had recognized that the vast majority of UFO and paranormal researchers were male, but never truly understood the scope of what that meant. I took a sip of my coffee and then immediately contacted Erica Lukes.

Lukes replied quickly to my messages and informed me that it was a huge problem. She told me about her experiences with various men in the field making sexist remarks about her in private and in public. Her personal dealings with a particular paranormal radio show host caused significant issues for her, both professionally and emotionally. She suggested that I speak to other women in the field, as she knew of several others who have had similar issues.

A curious question crossed my mind as I began making inquiries. How could a community, which engages in regular discussion concerning aliens, take issue with something so mundane as genitalia? However, the longer one roams around with UFO researchers, zealots, enthusiasts and junkies, one begins to realize that some within the UFO community are far from rational. It became clear very quickly that other women in the UFO community were experiencing harassment and unfair treatment due to their gender.

---

[12] Damante, Mike. *Erica Lukes details 'UFOs: The Lost Evidence,' obstacles in the field.* Punk Rock and UFOs Blog. June 9, 2017. https://www.punkrockandufos.com/blog/2017/6/9/erica-lukes-details-ufosthe-lost-evidence-obstacles-in-the-field

[13] Ibid.

I wish to present three particular individuals and some of the experiences they've had regarding discrimination within a ufological and Fortean framework.

Cheryl Costa is a researcher and author. Her book, co-authored by her wife, Linda Miller Costa, the *UFO Sightings Desk Reference: United States of America 2001—2015*, showcases the sighting data across all fifty states. She was also awarded the 2018 UFO Researcher of the Year at the International UFO Congress. She explained that ufology is basically an "all-boys club." She informed me that "the vast majority of speakers at UFO conferences are male," and that

"many men seem to have this idea that women in UFO research have nothing to contribute." She explained that women tend to look at things differently from men, especially regarding the UFO enigma. At one conference, she overheard a male researcher remark, "'These women are pushing serious researchers out of speaking slots.'"

Costa elaborated on some personal issues she has faced. She explained that her work is often not taken seriously, she was ignored during panel discussions and her conference talks were scheduled during the worst time slots. She was once informed that her research is "useless." During an investigation in which she was the lead, she was told that she was being "bitchy."

Susan Demeter St Clair, like Costa, has been involved in the UFO community for a long time. Her blog, *Out of My Mind's Eye*, is a collection of her work, and she is also a contributing writer to Paranormal Inquiry and Studies Canada, and her work is also featured in the book, *UFOs: Reframing the Debate*.

St. Clair expressed her thoughts to me in an e-mail:

> Anyone who has spent any quality time researching UFO experience will note the lack of diversity within the ranks of those who represent the most well-known authorities on the subject. Ufology currently is, and primarily always has been, the proverbial 'old boys' school:' male and white. This not only contributes to a very narrow view of the topic, it also subjects ufology to the same issues inherent with other male dominated fields of study, mainly sexism.

In 1999, when attending a MUFON symposium, she asked one of the conveners of the event who was a local MUFON investigator, about the process of joining the organization. He ignored her and called her "blondie" when he thought she was out of earshot.

St. Clair, even today, still has to deal with these issues. She stated:

> Twenty-one years after I joined the UFO discourse I participated in a groundbreaking book called *UFOs: Reframing the Debate*. It honors for me to be included with colleagues who, I feel, are the current top minds within our shared field of study. It has been pointed out to me that I am the only female essayist to contribute by a well-meaning fellow researcher; he said to me "You represented your gender well." This problem of gender bias and sexism is not a problem stemming only out of ufology. It's ultimately a problem of division of power in society. Our field of study is at best fringe and counter cultural, and where those who hold the power ultimately control the narrative and discussion...We have a long way to go.

Allison Jornlin is a Fortean researcher from Wisconsin. She expressed concern to me that while she could name dozens of male UFO researchers and writers, perhaps only a handful of female ones came to mind. Her greatest concerns focus on how she has been treated by certain men in the community.

One particular incident centered around a 2016 and 2017 string of alleged sightings of the famous Fortean creature, the Mothman, in Chicago, investigated by a team of researchers dubbed the Chicago Phantom Task Force. While her investigations into the sightings were initially positive, with members of the task force thanking her for her service and even sending messages of concern for her safety, things began to turn when she began to question some of the witness' accounts. Noticing some issues with claims made by the witnesses, Jornlin began to express some skepticism. One member of that task force messaged others stating, "I want to slap her!"

She writes:

> ...it seems a female like myself either needs to be protected from physical violence or treated violently. However, there is no middle ground, where this female should be allowed to stand on her own.

Jornlin explained that her YouTube channel has also received a few comments that were questionable. She explains:

> Most commenters have been respectful. However, some have pointed out the physical attributes of myself or other female researchers featured in the videos. One commenter remarked, "Hey, I just want to say you

women are doing an awesome job and no disrespect, but you have very voluptuous breast [sic]."

Jornlin discussed with me one other incident concerning a specific researcher who leads a paranormal investigation group in West Michigan. Jornlin informed me that he was a viewer of her YouTube channel, and that he added her as a friend on Facebook. He asked her if she desired to investigate the paranormal professionally and even offered a potential slot to speak at a paranormal conference. The man followed up by sending her pictures of his penis.

In complete shock, she blocked him and "in near panic struggled to delete the photos from [her] phone as [she] reported for work."

She asked that I not publish his name. Jornlin concluded our discussions with the following insights:

This would be a laughing matter if my gender wasn't always a consideration. I never know if someone is really interested in my ideas, just thinks I'm hot, or has more predatory intentions. Everything I do seems automatically sexualized just because I happen to be a woman. Is what I'm wearing too sexy? Would something more buttoned-down cause me to be taken more seriously? Or should I be using my sex appeal to gain attention for my work and take advantage of the fact that there are few women in the field? Doesn't every Mulder need a Scully? Is that my way into this competitive field? Am I just being too sensitive, too guarded, not guarded enough? If I appear with a man on video or collaborate with a man on research, will our findings be attributed to us equitably or will I have to fight for credit? Am I just being paranoid, a hysterical woman, playing the sexism card to get undue attention?

Male researchers in the field generally do not have to consider these questions, and it is undoubtable that many female researchers have asked similar questions.

I am a man writing about the experience of women. The irony is not lost on me. However, as this book concerns itself with the UFO subculture, this topic is one of great concern to many within the field, both women and men alike. My intention, here, is not to come to a conclusion as to why sexism and discrimination exist within the UFO community, nor why it exists in broader culture. There is no question that gender politics and issues seem to be everywhere. Rather, my intention is to shed light upon some of the issues that have arisen for women within the field. Furthermore, the UFO community is relatively silent on this issue. Clearly, silence is no longer an option.

Dr. Brenda Denzler did a series of surveys concerning this issue and published them in her book, *The Lure of the Edge; Scientific Passions, Religious Beliefs and the Pursuit of UFOs*. She found that roughly 56% of the UFO community were men and 44% were women.[14] While these numbers have undoubtedly changed since her surveys were done, it shows that there is no significant divide between those who take interest in the subject of UFOs. Denzler points out that the divide exists amongst individuals in the field who are published or promoted as "experts." She notes that in surveys done between 1995 and 1997, at twenty-one UFO related conferences, 80% of the invited speakers were men, and that the highest regarded periodicals regarding the subject, 87% of the articles written were by men.[15]

Denzler points out that one particular category within the UFO community does favour women: that of the abductee. According to her surveys, roughly 58% of abductees were women. She notes, however, that the vast majority of authors who pen books and articles concerning abduction are men, and that women are more likely to tell their own stories and be published by smaller presses than males, who tell the stories of others and enjoy support from larger publishing houses.[16]

While this data is decades old, it is telling that no one has done such a survey since. Furthermore, Denzler clearly points out that "despite the gendered dynamics of the UFO movement, gender is not an issue that gets explicit attention from students of the UFO phenomenon."[17] We must ask why.

The concept of the Other is nothing new to UFO discourse. Later, in Part 2 of this book, I will explore the idea that the construct of the alien upsets the balance between us and them, that it challenges, if not erases, the arbitrary rigidity of structural dichotomies; in other words, it creates anti-structure where male and female are separate, but require the other for their own definitions. Sarah Kember, a media professor at the University of London, suggests that the *alien* in

---

[14] Denzler, Brenda. *The Lure of the Edge: Scientific Passions, Religious Beliefs, and the Pursuit of UFOs*. University of California Press. 2001, 165

[15] Ibid.

[16] Ibid, 166

[17] Ibid.

feminist critique has always been the "ultimate outsider."[18] The alien as construct counters discrimination, be it racial or gender or even species. She compares the alien's place to that of "the monster" in Shelley's *Frankenstein*. However, Kember surmises that "the alien in feminist theory will continue to invoke a story, the story of switching sides … and to recognise as fallacy the idea that there are sides to be switched."[19]

What Kember ultimately arrives at in her deconstruction is that the alien is not actually an outsider, but "ingested" and connected to our ontology, "entangled" with the subject.[20] That is, one does not need to look to the stars or to UFOs to see the alien; rather, that outsider is within. However, this internalizing of the Other causes anxiety. It invokes social and cultural anxieties that the borders we've established, particularly around gender, are illusory. That is perhaps one of the most frightening aspects of *the outsider*: not that they do not belong but, rather, there is no place to belong to. In other words, the *alien as outsider* eliminates those constructs.

We must ask ourselves, as the UFO community, is this erasure of barriers the root cause of the issues of gender politics in UFO discourse? For some, perhaps it is. However, as a subculture, is there not a predisposition to understand already that certain truths are not true at all? Look at the collective narratives, which the UFO community deals with on a regular basis. Surely, gender is nothing compared to political conspiracies, alien visitation, and a phenomenon that regularly defies laws of physics, ethics, and reality itself. Or perhaps, in dealing with the UFO phenomenon, where no boundaries are sacred, certain illusions are maintained to retain some sense of social order?

It is in the very *uncanny* nature of UFOs themselves that the UFO community, or at least certain members of it, attempt to retain some semblance of a contrived social order. That is to say, some individuals within the community are unable to let go of the illusion; they prefer it to the reality—or rather, unreality—that the phenomenon brings with it. As anthropologist Susan Lepselter argues that the UFO phenomenon forces us to "enter inside those structures of…class, race and gender" simply to notice that "they don't stay put on their own foundations."[21]

---

[18] Kember, Sarah. "No humans allowed? The alien in/as feminist theory." *Feminist Theory*. 12(2), 184.

[19] Ibid.

[20] Ibid, 196

[21] Lepselter, Susan. The License: Poetics, Power and The Uncanny. in *E.T. Culture: Anthropology in Outerspaces*. Duke University Press. 2005, 145

Included in the Appendix is an essay written by Allison Jornlin. It presents the historical account of the first paranormal researcher who just so happened to be a woman. I will not say more, as Jornlin's work can speak for itself. However, it must be noted that Jornlin's subject, Catherine Crowe, also underwent significant prejudice and discrimination. That was over two centuries ago. From a cultural perspective, especially for a culture that looks to the stars and the future for insight and inspiration, it is curious that gender still plays a role in dictating one's value within the discourse.

The UFO community is forced by the phenomenon to enter the gap, the in-between, what Lepselter calls a "liminal space"[22] where hegemonic social structures, such as gender, come into conflict with a world view that simultaneously understands those structures to be illusions. The issue that arises is that "experience becomes slippery,"[23] the liminality of the UFO phenomenon and its inherent effect on the UFO community "denaturalizes dominant histories" and imagines "ghostly pasts and potential futures." This may very well be why some individuals within the community struggle to cope with women's engaging with ufological discourse, and why the topic of gender politics remains undiscussed. These may be phantoms they fear, or perhaps, they want to hold on to something stable and comfortable. Those who engage in bashing women, sexist comments or retaining systems of gender discrimination within the field, are simply unable and unwilling to find themselves in the gap of the subculture. They are unable to fathom that they themselves and the social order around them is the actual outsider, the true Other. The urge, then, is to fall back upon a safety net; to create false illusions of Otherness where it does not and fundamentally cannot exist.

Lepselter concludes that we are left with a "license to imagine."[24] Indeed, this is in the only way to move beyond these arbitrary structures and closed mindedness. Perhaps some members of the UFO subculture are simply unprepared to do so. It is odd that certain men are more willing to accept an extraterrestrial, and not a member of their own species. The question this begs then is obvious; if these individuals, these men, lack imagination, do they have any business engaging with a phenomenon that demands it?

---

[22] Ibid.

[23] Ibid, 147

[24] Ibid.

CHAPTER 6

Mundus Imaginalis

I wish to return back to Amy, and her strange encounters. Being a writer, she wrote down her interpretation of these mysterious events for me, and it is published in this book as a record of her engagement with the phenomenon. The next chapter is Amy's essay. It is not a formal recounting of the several mysterious events, which began to invade her quiet farming life; rather, it is her attempt to reason out why these events occurred.

Before we get to Amy's essay, I want to note a few points here.

First, we see a curious connection that exists between the seeking of the phenomenon, and the phenomenon's manifesting itself. In his ground-breaking work *The Invisible College*, Jacques Vallée argues that "Contact between human percipients and the UFO phenomenon occurs under conditions controlled by the latter. Its characteristic feature is a constant factor of absurdity...[25]

After I first spoke with Amy, and decided to look into her UFO sightings, the more sightings she began to have. After Jesse and I visited her home, there was another increase in sightings. With every new sighting, Amy would send me an e-mail. There was one point where I had ten new messages in my inbox, and five were from her. While one could argue that this is merely "wishful thinking" or some sort of

---

[25] Vallée, Jacques. *THE INVISIBLE COLLEGE*: What a Group of Scientists Has Discovered About UFO Influences on the Human Race (Kindle Locations 536-538). Anomalist Books. Kindle Edition.

confirmation bias, Amy has nothing to gain from these encounters, which seem, honestly, to frighten her. Furthermore, aspects of her story do, as Vallée suggests, seem *absurd*. However, Amy is not the first witness ever to report highly strange encounters, and, indeed, reality is often stranger than fiction. For Amy, there seems to be a correlation between the continued search for answers and the phenomenon itself. What we have yet to grasp fully is why.

Secondly, there seems to be a connection between her UFO encounters and what parapsychologists commonly refer to as *psi*. While there is debate over the very existence of psi in mainstream scientific circles, and disagreement over what exactly psi is, for the purposes of this book, basically it encapsulates a wide variety of mental phenomena, such as telepathy, psychokinesis and remote viewing. For more information regarding psi, I recommend reading *Real Magic: Ancient Wisdom, Modern Science, and a Guide to the Secret Power of the Universe* by Dr. Dean Radin.

Jacques Vallée points out:

> The key to an understanding of the phenomenon lies in the psychic effects it produces (or the psychic awareness it makes possible) in its observers. Their lives are often deeply changed, and they develop unusual talents with which they may find it difficult to cope.[26]

Amy recounts dreams in her story, which foretell of great doom and violence, where cities and highways erupt into chaos. Then, other dreams where she and a stranger walk in a field where there exists total peace and harmony, a world free from conflict. These dreams began only after her experiences. Are these merely dreams of an active imagination, a creative writer's mind, or is Amy engaged in perceiving information and data from a distant place and time, or perhaps something well beyond our understanding? Furthermore, Amy also claims that her intuition, her ability to understand a situation without directly reasoning it out, has also become sharpened. What can only be described as a sixth sense, a gut feeling that seems to be right more than it is wrong.

As philosopher and author Dr. Michael Grosso points out, Carl Jung believed that UFOs were "part of a collective death and rebirth

---

[26] Vallée, Jacques. *THE INVISIBLE COLLEGE*: What a Group of Scientists Has Discovered About UFO Influences on the Human Race (Kindle Locations 533-535). Anomalist Books. Kindle Edition.

experience."[27] Perhaps Amy's dreams are a prediction for the end of a technological or materialist future and the witnessing of a rebirth to some more natural state for humanity? Or, perhaps they are nothing but the machinations of the mind. This is all speculation, at least for now. Grosso also points out that the UFO experience may come from a source both outside and inside simultaneously:

> In one sense [they] originate from 'outside' our personal world but also from 'inside' our collective mental life... a zone of being that fuses objective and subjective realms but that is neither, entirely or exclusively... the *Mundus Imaginalis*.[28]

I want briefly to explore the term *Mundus Imaginalis* as it appears multiple times in the book. Henry Corbin was a French philosopher and theologian whose expertise rested in the study of Islam. During his academic career, he was introduced to the writings of the 12th century Persian mystic and philosopher, Suhrawardi. Corbin was heavily influenced by his work and used it to develop further his understanding of an ancient concept, which he personally called the *Mundus Imaginalis*.

Simply put, Corbin suggested that our normal material world—what we typically call *reality*, and what we use our five senses to perceive—is merely one realm of a more complicated landscape. The more complex realm, the intelligible world, first formally postulated by Plato but expanded upon by other philosophers such as René Descartes and Immanuel Kant, is where our non-physical intellect and consciousness resides: in other words, the place where the thoughts and reason come from in our minds. Corbin theorized that there exists a middle ground, what he called the "intermediate world" or "mundus imaginalis," which connects the worlds of the physical senses and the world of our intellect. He wrote that "it is a world whose ontological level is above the world of the senses and below the pure intelligible world; it is more immaterial than the former and less immaterial than the latter."[29]

Corbin argued that this middle realm, this imaginal world, was where our imagination came to be rooted. From this gap in-between

27 Grosso, Michael. *Experiencing the Next World Now.* Simon and Schuster. 2004, 202.

28 Ibid, 204.

29 Corbin, Henri. *Mundus Imaginalis, or the Imaginary and the Imaginal.* 1964. https://hermetic.com/moorish/mundus-imaginalis

worlds, our imagination would find very real things and experiences. He explained that the "forms and shapes" in this realm do not exist in the same way that they exist in our material world. Nor can they exist in the purely intelligible world, the world of pure thought or reason, as they do have "extension and dimension, an 'immaterial' materiality" which is related to our sensory world, but in possession of their own "corporeality and spatiality."[30] In other words, this imaginal realm is a real place with real things in it, but those things are very different from what we are used to in our everyday lives. It is the gap between our daily world and the world of the mind. It is the realm of ghosts, where things are both physical and metaphysical, real and mythological.

Is Amy being granted access to this realm in the gaps? Were her strange experiences caused by a seeping out of this *mundus imaginalis* and manifesting in the physical realm? Are her dreams and intuition being honed by a conduit to this nebulous gap between worlds? Are all experiencers and UFO witnesses seeing the forays of the bizarre into our reality? Again, we can only speculate.

Finally, Amy's experiences have totally reshaped her perception of the world around her. It seems to have brought together in her not only aspects of fear and love, disconnection and attachment, and an enlightened hope for the future, but also dark dreams foreshadowing great destruction. George P. Hansen, author of *The Trickster and The Paranormal*, argues that the UFO phenomenon itself has aspects, which resemble the archetypical trickster as it moves between boundaries and disrupts established dichotomies and dualities. It must be pointed out that Amy, as a witness to these phenomena, has herself become a boundary crosser. While her experiences bring great confusion, they also bring peace. What we see in Amy's story is a breaking down of dualisms. While this may very well be the domain of Hansen's trickster, the ghost is perhaps a better interpretation. Tricksters play with dualisms; they poke and prod at them, but they do not dismantle them like the ghost does. Her UFO experience, and potential contact with beings in her dreams, seem to remove the polarized states only to place her firmly in a middle place, the gap, where these dualistic states can exist in symbiosis.

As another UFO experiencer once explained to me, the phenomenon is "...a presentation. Kabuki theater at some level. Always presenting itself as just out of reach but telling you constantly 'You are not alone.'"

---

[30] Ibid.

It was the "Kabuki" part, which gave me pause. The root verb, *ka-buku*, which is thought to be the origin of the term Kabuki, roughly translates to "unordinary" in English. The general interpretation of Kabuki theatre is that it is typically weird or strange: in other words, it leans towards the odd. Is this what Amy is dealing with? What all self-professed UFO witnesses, experiencers, abductees and contactees are dealing with? Is the UFO as object, and even the extraterrestrial as *Other*, a sort of anomalous performance attempting to attract on-lookers and vying for attention? Perhaps. What seems to be missing, however, in this theatre of the uncanny, is the fourth wall.

What we must conclude from Amy's tale—from her personal mythology, which is both reflective and reflexive—is that the UFO phenomenon is not something she merely observed, but that also observes her. There is no fourth wall, and, indeed, it often requires significant audience participation. It not only appears but it also distorts and adjusts ideology and paradigm. It challenges, if not totally removes, the foundations of reality. Amy may have had hidden or latent parapsychological abilities before her encounters, but something about her encounters seems to have shown them to her. Vallée refers to the phenomenon as being absurd. If the experiencer above is right, then the phenomenon engages in absurdist theatre. It held up a mirror and allowed Amy to peer into some ghostly apparition of herself, a simulacrum of the self, which is essentially identical and totally different: a self that is no longer limited by the illusory boundaries established by her cultural and social self. A self that not only dwells in the physical world and the intelligible world, but one that is also communion with a middle ground, an imaginal world: the *mundus imaginalis*.

The upcoming chapter will present Amy's interpretation of the events, and how they have affected her. These are her words and ideas, unedited, and I will let the readers interpret them as they see fit.

CHAPTER 7

The Startling Truth

By A.J. McCormick

~

I have learned a miraculous truth: UFOs exist.
My astronomical outpost has been, for my numerous sightings to date, the rural Manitoba acreage I call home. The land is flat, the sky big. I call it Paradise. Here I love life and nature. I am a master of tranquility. But within the last several years, strange objects in these skies have clouded the fine simplicity I enjoy.

I have never been compelled to seek out UFOs. They have sought out me. The question I ask myself is why? Am I a beacon to alien life forms because I love my planet and care about humanity? Do I emit a certain aura that only they can see from above? What is it that has attracted them to me?

My sightings have utterly transformed me. Our massive, mysterious universe is an eternal, inevitable relationship between function and form and I am not one to criticize, only contemplate. It's necessary in that contemplation that, as the UFO spectator, I must fully participate in such strangeness by means of the UFO phenomenon and its will acting upon my mental and physical being. The complex truth about UFOs and their effect on me have yet to be truly understood by experts in the field. I feel at times all alone, not blessed to have sightings/encounters but shocked. I am left puzzled, fumbling for answers, sometimes weak in the legs just thinking about such advanced cultures that I have viewed travelling through our skies.

In seeing these crafts, extraordinary airships, celestial phenomena that appear to be operated by unknown intelligences, I have ultimately been provoked, scared, and had my senses deranged.

I am certain, with regard to one of my sightings, a particularly terrifying one, which took place about 11:30 one autumn morning in 2016. It appeared out of nowhere in the northern sky on September 28th. I noticed it only because I was throwing a ball into the air and catching it. It was late morning before lunch. The sky was clear, and a light breeze blew. I couldn't miss the object, which was large with a rounded bottom and domed top.

It was travelling nearer to my property. To start with this terrified me because I had no idea what it was, and I dreaded to think that perhaps it would come down in my yard. The more I watched it advance, the more it grew in size. Its form became more evident as it got closer. My heart was racing. I was so scared. I am doomed, I thought. This thing must be able to see me. What will happen to me? Why is there no one else around to see this? Why am I alone with something so foreign, so unexplainable?

The fear within me, cold as lead and hot as lava, released from me like speeding bullets. I couldn't control it. I hyperventilated at times. The object was soon going to be right over me so I moved to conceal myself in front of my barn's doorway. It can't see me here, I thought, but no, it could. I sensed strongly that it could and that there was no use hiding from it. They (whoever they were) weren't stupid. I don't know what will happen to me, be it good or bad, but I must try to get a photo of this. I had to do this, to show others. I felt as though it was my duty.

I was still in panic mode but I pulled my phone out of my pocket and got it ready. But how will they react if I take their photo? What if they get angry and do something terrible to me? These questions raced through my mind. As ridiculous as I must have appeared, I crouched down and just aimed my phone at the object. I didn't have the guts to look at it while I snapped a photo. Oh, dear God! I said to myself. It's nearly overhead now! It was so huge as it drew nearer in the sky! At the same time, it did not appear so evident as an airplane would. I could see it, but it seemed a bit misty. The bottom half of it was solid, that I could see. The top half was domed and more transparent with 'things' racing through it, almost like some kind of energy. Its entire color appeared to be white. I managed three photos but didn't know if I had captured its image because I was so nervous, shaking, and reluctant. The odd thing is that, even though I can describe the object almost directly above me and my property, I can't remember its passing directly overhead. By all accounts, it had to because of its path direction. But when I think about it, there is a break there, as though in time, where I'm standing further away from my barn and the object is leaving further off to the southwest in the clear blue sky. When I watched it vanish into nothing, I thought: that's impossible! I should definitely have been able to see it much, much further on. I felt completely helpless, knowing for certain I had no choice in anything: to flee; to sit; to yell. And yet, as intimidating as that was, a weird sense of calm prevailed within me as I watched it sail slowly across the blue sky and vanish. I was even smiling! It was all so very strange. I was anxious to tell my husband about it when I got home that night from work.

Why had this incredible, unidentifiable object invaded me so deeply, emotionally, I later wondered. It seemed to me to be exact in its movement and preparation for appearing before me; but for what purpose? As much as I was horrified to look at it, I was also mesmerized by it. My curiosity had the greatest panic attached to it. It was as though some fierce storm was about to hit and its large hail was going to injure me. The last thing that was ever on my mind was to get into my truck and drive away. That's what people normally do if they can, to flee from an intimidating situation. But I was glued to this object in some way. I would say I was "under the thumb" of this thing and, because of that, I was unable to think or react rationally.

It wasn't until the following day I realized that my phone calculated the photos were taken at 5:20 p.m. and not around 11:30 a.m. as I believed. I just didn't know how to comprehend this and asked my husband if my phone might give an incorrect time when taking a photo. "Never," he said. "They're always accurate."

I said nothing. I told no one. I denied it to myself, this discrepancy with the time. I remained silent about it for a long time, many months. I went over and over it in my mind, my encounter of that September day, never being able to make sense of it, feeling quite helpless about it. When I think about the encounter, what I endured emotionally and psychologically, it's as though I'm remembering someone else, that it wasn't actually me there but another body that looks just like me, as though my conscience is separated from my body, the two are disconnected. This is, to me, very disturbing. I was in denial, like a woman in denial of a sexual assault upon her. No, this can't be, I told myself.

In following weeks, I had multiple UFO sightings. Objects in different colors, sizes, shapes and speeds came over my property. My husband also saw a couple and watched one in silver through binoculars. I took more photos when able. I don't know what to make of this hotbed of UFO activity here. I'm a retired flight attendant and know my aircraft. None of these were airplanes or helicopters. Those do go over here, and I can certainly distinguish the differences.

So what do I make of this situation? A sensation of newness is produced that is having a positive relationship with my soul's particular energy. I'm not sure if this is a good or bad thing but I certainly feel it and perhaps because I'm ultra-receptive to begin with. It's like having an extra sense, that my soul is being governed by it while simultaneously my mind fights it as though it is an immense weakness of observed fact that I should dispose of. And, yes, I have tried to dispose of this sensation. Clearly, I cannot. It seems it's there to stay, an expression of truth in technical terms, perhaps one bearing a relationship to that sublime power to which our Creator projects. I am content with this sensation, but I'm also disgruntled by the violation, hence my reason for trying to dispose of it. I must accept it for what it is, whatever that may be. Those who know me well admire me in my capacity for belief, which is as extraordinarily vivid as that of doubt in others.

A Close Encounter of the Third Kind?

I have seen mysterious objects in different shapes, colors, sizes, and speeds that have forced an entrance into my eyes, slowly at first then patiently penetrating every fiber of my being. Thousands of sensations have rippled through me or stabbed me, telling me yes, I've enriched my earthly existence but if only I could help to solve those unprecedented mysteries of the universe!

Locked within the blinding numbness of my sighting/encounters are my fears, panic, terror, and stress but, still all the while, I realize I am witness to rare spectacles that are far more incredible in those moments than the smell and movement of horses in my neighbor's field.

It is a cruel punishment in having multiple sightings. It's taxing on my mental and physical being. The spontaneous expectation of seeing a UFO of celestial vitality is indeed remarkable but I am left with questions and virtually no answers. I do feel, however, that I am blessed with some strange form of wisdom. It feels deep and timeless, a unique energy pulsating within my brain at all times. But naturally I cannot begin to decipher what form of wisdom this is, except that possibly it is linked with my memory. If this unusual form of wisdom is a gift, then my memory is the recipient because I have moments in which I remember something related to the cosmos. When I recall it, wisdom is somehow attached to it, as though to say I have been given a gift to make me as intellectually wise as possible.

I have a recollection of darkness and sound within profound stillness. I am surrounded by the vastness of outer space to which I am deliberately dedicated. I am exposed to something outstanding in the farthest depths of space, some location that is pinnacle and I wonder if this is outer space's end or is it a wall bordering one cosmos on the next? I listen carefully to heavy churning sounds, understanding it is the sound of time as though time were alive and had a voice. I realize that, in this journey, I will go back to my own time and place because I have complete confidence and trust in those who brought me here. I am contented and at peace more than words can describe. My mind rejoices in these feelings. It's as though my intellect and senses are fused with all existing galaxies. In one way this particular strangeness seems to define my individuality. I am aware how precious my life is, how all life is. This is all I can recall of this encounter, unfortunately.

The Brain Connection

Once the harsh idea of seeing UFOs softens, and I guarantee it's temporary, I have to ask, to what future in an afterlife am I bound for? I can confirm there is an afterlife due to the fact I have witnessed ghosts of the dead on two occasions. Like UFO sightings, paranormal visions have also been debated a million times. No one knows for certain what exists until they see it with their own eyes. I should also note that, even at a distance too great for a spectator to be able to decipher or even comprehend his/her subject matter (I refer to UFOs or ghosts here), the curious phenomenon at hand will already have produced a rich and happy or sad impression upon the soul. The phenomenon at a distance can project its thought, stabilizing that connection to the brain. This has occurred in my own experience.

Without my ever seeing the phenomenon, one recent summer afternoon something was making a connection directly to my brain. The atmosphere's leaden calm felt intimidating as I watched a large, rare bird perched on an outbuilding. By all accounts the bird should have been annoyed by my presence. But, unlike nature, it was as still as a statue and unnerved. Minutes passed. How many I don't know. Afterwards the bird became alive and in motion. I took several pictures of it with my smartphone as it soared slowly by me. A profound, imperfect harmony linked the bird and atmosphere with me that I could not understand. I inspected the photos that evening only to discover a UFO in the fourth photo. I was shocked. It made sense to me, then, that I felt the way I did while unaware that a strange object hovered in the nearby sky space. I never laid eyes on the extraordinary craft, yet it devoured my very intellect and brushed all my senses with its own magical glaze.

My mind sinks into all this with a slow, uneasy rapture as it would sink into the ocean's horizon. I could easily become highly strung over this particular sighting/encounter, but I cudgel my brain, instead, in order to extract some formula, which may help me to deal properly with this. It's because the most incredible aspect of that fourth photo is that the UFO matches perfectly to a UFO in a painting composed three thousand years ago. I came upon the painting purely by accident shortly after this encounter while watching a televised documentary on ancient artworks depicting UFOs. Coincidence? I'm not so sure.

Have I inherited through these last few thousand years some sort of privilege? Was the rare bird, which I saw that day, there to protect me, like the bird associated with the Egyptian god Horus that had special protective powers and was often represented in artworks protecting and hovering over a Pharaoh? I am not convinced that my bird was supernaturally protecting me; of course one never knows, but life is fragile and is packaged with many mysteries, and I do appreciate the fortune I have gained in being one with nature while surviving the risks and labors of every day.

Fear

To deny I ever saw UFOs or ghosts would be like claiming my imagination had reached its full throttle. I can only repeat, with more conviction than ever, that my sightings and possible abductions were life-altering events. I have no desire to astonish anyone. I think it is a happiness to wonder what exists beyond our realm just as it is a happiness to dream. But it is the actual experience of what wonder has produced in me that, for the most part, has removed happiness.

Fear seems to be the strongest emotion within me most often. Fear agitates me, especially when my memory recalls my sightings. It has given me a dash of comfort, knowing that MJ and other experiencers in the UFO community have been there for me.

The entire visible universe is a storehouse of images and signs. There are just too many mysteries out there to which one's imagination can give place and value. For example, most recently I awakened abruptly and coherently to find some peculiar apparatus hovering above me. One could argue that I was dreaming. I'd prefer to accept that possibility rather than the alternative, which is the reality of a probe, a laser, a camera, a scope, an eye that was busy at work doing something to me—I could not identify it as anything I've ever seen. It had intelligence or was operated by intelligence because it discovered that I had acknowledged it and decided to leave, making a circular motion and vanishing. It wasn't large: about the size of a baseball. Again, fear set in.

Fear set in more so when, several nights afterwards, I awoke to my bedroom fully lit with bright white light that remained for several seconds and disappeared. I'm at the point where I fear the intensity of my own emotion. I appear to have acute awareness of such strange happenings that equal in strength to my fear. One thing I can rely on is the peace of mind I enjoy when I remember a specific dream I had many years ago. In this dream I walked calmly with a stranger across a field in darkness. Above us in the inky sky were UFOs travelling at great speeds, dashing here and there in no set pattern. Due to their swift movement I could not make out shapes of crafts, but they left fizzy trails in different colors. The stranger and I talked about how fantastic it was that the world was at complete peace, that it was safe enough to walk anywhere at any time, even in darkness. I never felt more content in my life when I awakened from that beautiful dream and remain contented to this day when recalling it.

Foreseeing Future Catastrophe: Psychic Awareness or Implanted Technology?

In weeks following my sightings/encounters, I had horrible dreams and visions foretelling catastrophe. These intense dreams at night, and visions during the days, involved vehicles travelling quickly on roads and parking lots and recklessly mowing down people. I awakened from the dreams shaken, exhausted and disgusted to no end. I wondered, how can I possibly have such dreams, and why when I would be peeling potatoes or doing laundry have similar visions?

In these dreams/visions I have seen people panicked and running for their lives from something awful: exactly what I didn't know. I only saw the injured and dead of all ages and races, their eyes staring in shock and horror into mine. I was unable to assist anyone. It seemed I could only witness urgency, dismay, and pleas for help. I watched these scenes unfold and felt deep pity and sadness. Have my UFO connections in some way cultivated these dreams/visions? Why would I be made to see such things, things that have actually become a reality in one form or another with recent terror attacks and massive movements of displaced refugees fleeing wars?

A woman in my own hometown was a victim in the 2017 Las Vegas shooting. I saw her several days before she travelled there and got shot. I had an incredibly odd feeling when I communicated with her but said nothing of course because I didn't know how to explain that feeling to her or to myself. I did not know she was travelling to Las Vegas when I saw her. I knew nothing of her plans. I only knew that weird feeling I got while seeing her before she left. She survived the shooting thankfully, but not without great pain and a long road to recovery after a bullet tore through her stomach. How does all this make me feel? Shocked to say the least, but, most of all, completely compassionate for all life on Earth.

Planets and Stars

It isn't hard to imagine that alien visitors have a presence on Earth. I do not know for certain, but is it possible? Of course. As curious as I am about where aliens are travelling from, I have also recently become uneasy while scanning the stars at night. This emotion startles me because I've always loved looking up to the starlit heavens. Why should one particular constellation bother me—and I mean so much that I must turn away quickly—while another one impresses me as being infinitely good? It's absurd that I feel like this and I tell myself so, yet I continue to feel as though I must turn away from certain stars because I cannot tolerate the sight of them. I have no explanation for this, other than whatever force is working within me is here to stay, it seems.

The Pentagram

I, personally, don't believe there is any differentiation between myself and the world I move through. That is to say I am, along with everyone else, attached like a limb to the complete universe. I know there is more to life than just this planet that we walk and breathe on. We cannot fathom the size of the universe, its beginning or end, because those boundaries don't exist. There must be something more out there, other life forms, or a form of unity with some other force that remains in waiting for us all when we leave the constraints of our physical beings.

Just as UFOs have marked fields and landscapes with mysterious symbols such as crop circles, it is ironic that one planet alone can mark the universe with another perfect symbol: the pentagram. Planet Venus draws this exquisite design in glorious flawlessness around the Sun every eight years as a result of its motion, touching all signs of the zodiacal constellations. While the Sun travels around Earth eight times, Venus will travel around the Sun thirteen times to make the pentagram.

Surprisingly, I have only just discovered this recently. This revelation was a stunning eye-opener for me because I have been sketching, doodling, drawing the pentagram for as long as I can remember, never knowing what it was all about. Why have I always been marking papers with pentagrams? Humans have given this symbol a history of its own. Pythagoreans used it to represent the five elements: Idea, Heat, Air, Earth, and Water. In Hebrew tradition, the pentagram is ascribed to Truth. In Celtic religions, it is mostly associated with femininity and knowledge. The pentagram signifies a range of things. I'm not sure which of them, if any, to believe in or if I believe at all.

But if Venus is creating a pentagram every eight years in the heavens, and I've unknowingly been sketching it all my life, then what am I to surmise? Since it also represents humanism and signifies man's relation to the cosmos and is seen as a guard against evil, I can't help being swayed by these features. These are positive things I can hold onto in my heart. Navigating my life on Earth has been, for the most part, challenging. Very little has come easily to me, yet I have seen more UFOs in a relatively short period of time than most people have seen in a lifetime. Behind the pageantry of their presence is a well-reasoned and serious purpose. This seems to be the most well-guarded secret of our time.

CHAPTER 8

Roy

Amy's story is similar to those of countless others who have experienced UFOs and episodes of high strangeness. It speaks to the ubiquitous nature of the phenomenon and that, regardless of its source, it changes the people involved. It becomes a social force, which not only embeds itself in the local legends and lore of a given geographic area, but also within people. It creates a culture of outsiders who no longer exist in our given "normal" reality, but in the gap between what is real and what isn't. They gain dual citizenship in a place that has no actual place. Whether we call it the *mundus imaginalis*, the realm of the trickster, or the haunting of a ghost, Amy and others like her have become part time dwellers of an undiscovered country.

Are all these stories actually *true*? Are the events they describe *real* in an objective sense? I do not know. Ultimately, while an answer would be compelling, it does not matter. These stories have embedded themselves into the world and become, for better or worse, an aspect of our common collective culture. The UFO, the alien, the ghost, the monster and the rest of the paranormal chorus have become, in some way, actualized. These concepts exist in our language and in our minds. Life has been breathed into them by the very people who experience them. Furthermore, this state of existence and nonexistence has created an entire culture of individuals who choose to engage with this phenomenon.

At the time of this book's publication, Amy has continued to experience odd events and encounters with UFOs. Her intuition has been sharpened, honed to a perfect edge, and she can sense *information* as if it is in the air. I never had reason to doubt Amy and her story. However, as this chapter will present, many stories exist within the subculture that problematize our assumptions regarding UFO witnesses and experiencers. Some individuals find peace in telling their stories. It becomes problematic when those individuals suffer from poor personal and mental health. Delusion, at times, can provide comfort when a survivor needs to disassociate from a painful experience. How does the community ethically move forward in continuing to pursue the phenomenon without compounding psychological harm upon experiencers who are not truly experiencers of something alien, but victims of very human trauma?

I want to tell another story now. I have spoken to countless UFO witnesses and individuals who allege alien visitation. These people and their experiences have become a complex system of faces and anecdotes, and, indeed, have become a series of living compartments in my mind—a curious collection of myths and legends, many of which still affect me to this day. Amy is one of those compartments. There are others. However, I will never forget the first time I sat down with someone to talk about his experiences, a man whom I will call Roy.

I will begin at the end. I am not a mental health professional; however, I believe that Roy was in need of mental health support and treatment. Was he being regularly abducted by extraterrestrials? I truly do not know. However, my instinct (for what it's worth) tells me that he was not. Was he carrying significant grief and pain due to the loss of his family? Yes. Is it possible that he created for himself a place to retreat, a gap between worlds, a realm where he was being victimized, instead of facing his own depression and anger? Yes. Upon reflection, I must ask myself if there is any difference between Roy's delusional retreat and the realm of real UFO stories. I do not know.

His wife and adult son left his life in early 2010. The separation was not amicable and very painful for Roy. He never disclosed the reason. I was informed about him in early 2011, well before I joined MUFON, but just as I was beginning to explore UFO culture. The case was given to me by a UFO researcher who knew I had interest in the subject. Roy's experiences began in mid-2010, after the departure of his family from his life, and carried on fairly regularly, and possibly still do today. I have not spoken to Roy since 2012.

I received an email from Roy in February of 2011 with a simple story. Roy's first abduction occurred around late March of 2010. Attached to the email was a photograph of the top of his head; there was a one-inch "incision" that sat on the crown of his scalp. He took that picture the morning after "they" took him the first time. He explained that this was not an implant site, but rather an injury from an electrode type device they used to render him unconscious. The device had an edge to it, that, when placed upon his head, created the injury. It then sent an electric shock through his system, and he blacked out. During every subsequent abduction, he would feel his legs tingle and then go numb. He said that this numbing feeling preceded each abduction experience, which occurred every two or three months. He would then sense the presence of multiple beings in the room, followed by an electric shock that would run through his body, and he would black out.

Each abduction experience was exactly the same and occurred at night while he was in bed: tingling and numbness in his extremities, feelings of being visited by multiple beings, a feeling of electric shock and then a loss of consciousness. He could not remember anything, he had no idea what these beings looked like nor had any idea why he was being targeted by them.

The case was intriguing to say the least, so I decided to ask Roy to meet me at a local coffee shop. I sent the picture of his head injury via email to a nurse friend of mine and asked her what could have caused such an injury. I did not mention Roy or his story. It read, simply:

"Hey! Check out this cut. What could cause this head injury?
Thanks,
M."

Roy and I met a few days after I received his first email. Roy looked tired, as if he'd not had a good night's sleep in a year. He looked to be in his late fifties, older than he actually was: a man who had been kicked so hard it knocked him over, and then kicked a few more times for good measure. His family was gone; he'd left his job and was living on disability payments due to a neck injury. He seemed broken.

I had many questions, all of which were answered honestly and truthfully. Roy was not a hoaxer, or, if he was, he had mastered it. The tone in his voice was exhausted and depressed, yet angry. He believed what was happening to him. He was afraid and alone. We spoke for more than an hour. He told me about his work and his neck injury. He spoke a little about his family, mainly his son of whom he was proud. He never went into detail about why his wife and son left him. He then got into his abduction experiences. They always happened at night, while he slept. He would wake up to that feeling in his legs and arms. It terrified him.

He had never seen his abductors, and the only confirmation he had was the device they placed on his head, on that first night, to deliver the initial shock. It was black, metallic, and had glowing lights on it. I asked him how they placed it on his head without giving themselves away. He told me that he did not know. He saw the device; it was held so close to his face that the light from it blinded him because the room was dark. He felt it touch his head but did not feel any pain from the incision. He then felt the shock and blacked out.

He told me about the frequency of the abductions and that he could recall being taken about 14 times, but he wasn't completely sure. He also let me know that he had suspicions that the entities recently began following him around.

Before Roy and I parted company after that meeting, he said something, which still bothers me to this day: "It's good that people like you exist. I just want this to stop."

I remember looking up at him, and pain ran through my heart. I had that sick feeling of pity in my stomach. I told him that I probably couldn't make it stop. I was just here to listen to his story and that there was nothing much I could do. He simply smiled: "We'll figure it out..."

At the time, the next words out of my mouth seemed normal, logical and they oozed common sense. I have become wiser with experience, but in 2011, I was brand new to the UFO community. I was totally unaware of their weight and the massive blow they dealt to his ego, self-esteem and feelings.

"Roy, have you seen a doctor? Maybe you should see a doctor."

"I thought you believed me." Roy was annoyed, maybe hurt. Probably both.

I explained that we needed to rule out other possibilities. What if this all was caused by anxiety or depression? What if his experiences were related to a mental health concern?

"I just need confirmation that there isn't something else going on before we ..."

Roy cut me off, "I get it. I've always thought I needed to be hypnotized. Maybe I will remember something."

That is not what I had meant, but I couldn't get a word in. He almost seemed manic. He assured me he would start looking for a hypnotherapist, told me he had to go, and walked out of the coffee shop.

My friend emailed me back about the head injury. We corresponded about it back and forth for a couple of days, and, when she learned that it occurred at night in bed, she guessed that the injury was caused by someone hitting their head on the headboard. Roy's bed did have a wooden headboard. It was perfectly reasonable that he was having nightmares or night terrors.

I thought I had a solution for Roy. Night terrors are often repetitive, bring on the same feelings, and can be a symptom of extreme stress. He was always in bed asleep when it happened, so what else could it be?

I've learned, through my forays into UFO culture, that this phenomenon is much more human than I thought initially. People place significant personal, and often spiritual, weight upon what they believe is happening to them. Suggesting anything contradictory can cause a visceral reaction. Roy's entire life, all he built for himself, walked out the door. His career, his health and his family were all gone. Something had to fill that void. Roy was terrorized by his abduction experiences, but it gave him purpose. It filled the emptiness left by a life that crumbled away; and sometimes pain is better than the thought of nothingness and meaninglessness.

It is impossible that every single case of alien abduction is objectively real. By sheer numbers alone, some cases must be caused by hallucinations and/or issues caused by poor mental health. I am of the belief that Roy was unwell. I have spoken to many other individuals who do not fall into the same category as Roy, whom I've gotten to know well, and whom I believe to be sound and to have experienced something totally anomalous. Roy needed a doctor, not a hypnotherapist, nor a ufologist.

Roy continued to send descriptions of his experiences and many photographs. He took photos of his bedroom with "orbs" hovering about, which clearly were dust particles. He sent other photos of his basement with more orbs that resembled dust. He sent a photo of a dog—a German shepherd—with bright yellow orbs surrounding it. None of these photos were compelling and they certainly weren't evidence of aliens or abduction. Roy sent me dozens of photos similar to this. I even began to receive short video clips of insects flying in front of the camera lens, which he claimed were small probes tracking his movements.

I regret what happened next, and I wish I could have mustered up the courage to simply tell Roy that he needed to seek professional care. We had been interacting for weeks, and I knew that whatever was going on, it was most likely not alien abduction. He then sent me a long e-mail explaining that he found a hypnotherapist in California who was willing to see him. He explained that she was an expert in alien abductions, and she has helped many people. Whoever this person was, she was clearly a confidence artist who bilked people out of their money. How does one become an "expert in alien abductions?" One cannot be an expert in unknowable things.

It was clear that Roy was experiencing some type of catharsis from this experience and from the fact that someone was listening to his story. He had someone in his corner. I, like a coward, decided to not tell Roy my thoughts. The dozens of photos he sent me, he saw something there. Perhaps it was hope or fear or both. Those photographs were a window to a world where he was no longer alone, but something, even something alien, was becoming part of his life. While he was lying in his bed, taking photographs in the middle of the night, he was capturing something real. In those dark shadowy corners, he knew he was no longer alone.

Several weeks later, Roy sent me his final e-mail. The alien abduction hypnotherapist expert in California was too expensive. He found another therapist closer to home on a popular UFO website's forum. He and his brother were going to Toronto to meet this person. He explained that he was going to keep me posted on what this hypnotherapist found.

I did not reply. I never let Roy know what I thought about his case and I chalk that up to inexperience and cowardice. Doing this kind of work, you meet people from many walks of life. Roy had no evidence of his dealings with otherworldly beings, but he was being taken away by something. Pain, loss, and depression are much more potent than any alien visitor.

It is curious that I am haunted by this. I regret the way this all happened with Roy, and it pains me that he may still be out there dealing with this conflict. I once asked my friend, author and colleague Ryan Sprague if he believed that experiencers of the phenomenon held some privileged position in the UFO community. Did I, as someone who has never had a paranormal experience, have the right to engage in UFO discourse? His answer was very wise.

"It is important to have both sides. We must be respectful towards each other. Always Critical. But respectful."

I was critical of Roy's claims because I knew he had convinced himself that there existed no other possible cause to his experiences. That being said, he had not seen a doctor. In the end, I do not believe he wanted a solution. He did not want this reality to go away, no matter what he told me. If it did, he would have suffered loss again. He would have been alone.

At the time of this publication, I have been unable to locate or speak to Roy. His phone number is no longer in service. He does not respond to e-mails. He has no contact with his previous employer. He has vanished and become a ghost in his own right. I am haunted by my memories of him, some hastily jotted notes in an old notebook and a few megabytes of e-mails and photographs.

Although I question the objective validity of his experiences, I cannot question his *personal knowing* of those experiences. For the lack of a better term, he *believes* they happened. He has created his own ghost story out of necessity. Perhaps Roy's experiences are more real than previously understood. If the mythologies that surround a real UFO phenomenon are any indication, we as a community have also generated our own ghost stories. Are we simply afraid of being alone? Do we find solace in the company of space aliens or mystical beings? Does it matter if they are peaceful or frightening? *Anything* may simply be better than *nothing*.

The more I interact with the UFO community, the more people I interview and befriend, the more I realize how little I truly know, and how little the rest of the community knows. There are no UFO experts, nor are there experts regarding aliens or interdimensional beings. True expertise in this subculture is becoming comfortable with the fundamental principle that no one knows a damn thing; if they say they do, they are lying, delusional or trying to sell you something.

Roy, in his odd and weird way, has provided me with an education. He has convinced me that I must remain open-minded to the possibility that what I *think* may not necessarily be true. Does that change my gut feeling towards Roy's mental health? No. Does it allow me to consider the possibility that my gut is wrong? Yes, and I have learned to be fine with that. Roy's ghost has shown me that I, and the UFO community in general, stand with our feet in two worlds, the normal and the bizarre. That being said, I hope Roy, wherever his current haunt is, will find some peace. Lastly, it also taught me that UFOs and aliens manifest not only in our skies, but in our minds as well. Roy, in my opinion, was experiencing a psychological event, and not a real objective one. Not all UFO reports, and not all stories of alien abduction and contact, are true. It begs the question; how many other paranormal reports are products of the mind? How many individuals shield themselves from real problems and pain with reports of flying saucers and little grays with their large black eyes?

I must be cautious. While I am convinced that Roy was dealing with issues regarding his mental health, and his alien experiences were manifestations of those issues, I am in no way qualified to diagnose him. Why do I believe Amy is telling me the "truth" and not Roy? I admit that I have no evidence. All I have is my gut feeling, a hunch. I believe, but do not know. However, belief does not make it true or factual. Roy may indeed have had these bizarre events happen to him. Herein lies another ghost: just when you think you know, the phantom pulls the firm foundation out from under you and down you fall back into confusion.

Roy, and others like him, are not the only ghosts who muddy our interpretation of the UFO phenomenon. The UFO community seems to be made up of many ghosts, one of whom began to haunt my life in early 2017. His name is Richard Doty.

CHAPTER 9

The Ghost of Richard Doty

Personal Message Transcript with a fellow UFO researcher

*"Hey. I have a question. What do you know about Richard
Doty?"*
"Why?"
"I want to interview him for my book."
"You can't trust anything he says. You know that right?"
"That's what people say, yep."
*"He is retired, but he seems to be involved again. He can
probably still contact people in his old job. Don't bring me up
in this..."*
"Ok..."
*"Whatever he says is a mix of truth and fiction. You won't be
able to double check any of it. Please keep my name out of
this."*
"I will. Don't worry. You seem worried"
"No. I'm fine."
"You sure?"
"Be careful. I can't stress that enough."
"Ok. Now I'm worried. Why am I worried?"
"He knows what he's doing. Been doing it a long time."
"I just want to talk about his role in the UFO subculture.

I don't really care about the UFO thing. Or the whole
disinformation thing. I care more about him."
"You are going to get played."
"Damn."

End Message Transcript

You meet a lot of interesting people in the UFO community, but no other individual is lionized and demonized like Richard Doty. He is the first to tell you that he is not, and has never been, a part of that community, and, to some extent, he is correct. One UFO researcher, whom I will not name, told me that he is "the most loathed man in all of ufology." However, he does not seem to be bothered by it. When I spoke to him for the first time, he informed me that, "the UFO community is going to the shithouse." Doty is an outsider in the UFO world, yet he is an integral part of it. Ironically, he is an outcast among outcasts who have cast him out.

Doty feels as though he has been treated unfairly by the community, painted as a "persona non grata" because he knows the truth, and when that truth does not jive with "the experts," they purposefully tear him down and discredit him. They paint him as a disinformation agent and a liar. Whether he is or not, he has not only had significant influence upon the UFO community, he embodies the *Otherness* of it. While the UFO community may paint him as a villain, Doty, whether he likes it or not, is a symbolic representation of the subculture and the UFO phenomenon itself; he is an archetype within, what Jung calls, "the living myth" that is UFO discourse. It is simple to dismiss him as a villain within the history of ufology, but this approach is lazy, and it does not address that decades later, he is still haunting the subcultural landscape of ufology. The man is a ghost who dwells in the gap between truth and fiction, and his specter raises a startling truth for the UFO community: the UFO discourse is embodied by what Doty archetypically represents—a continued spinning of cultural paradigms, ideology and mythology.

Doty's story is complex and mythological in nature. It has no formal beginning and has yet to end. Much like the UFOs and extraterrestrials that Doty alleges to have seen, one must come to terms with the gap between real and imagined. Carl Jung pointed out an inherent problem with the UFO phenomenon: was "primary perception" of the UFO "followed by a phantasm or, conversely, a primary fantasy originating in the unconscious invaded by the conscious mind with illusions and visions?"[31]

We see in Doty the ghost of the UFO subculture: he is that which haunts, causing ideologies and paradigms to form, but his myth-making is also being influenced by ideology and paradigm.

Within the strange confines of the ufological historical narrative, how is it that Doty still influences the contemporary UFO culture? Was it his actions in the 1980s, or the effects of his actions, which now dwell in the collective unconscious of the UFO subculture? In other words, is the UFO community still reeling from Doty's alleged historical misdeeds, or is Doty still haunting the community? The legend of Richard Doty, that collective mythos which has formed around him, exists because it has discursive impact and does not exist because much of it dwells more as lore than actual fact. More bizarre than Doty, the mythology around him, too, is a ghostly shadow whose presence shapes much of the modern paradigms that have become the UFO narrative.

Within UFO circles, to suggest that Doty's name is famous is perhaps an understatement. A huge portion of UFO lore over the last couple of decades somehow has his name attached to it, regardless of his involvement or not. While one can argue that Doty's background in Air Force counterintelligence may have had him involved in some shady espionage, he became the boogey man of UFOs when a man named Paul Bennewitz entered his life. Whatever information Doty may have fed to the UFO community before, his interactions with Bennewitz are really what people know him for. As William Moore, who will become important later in this chapter, stated in front of a crowded room at the Aladdin Hotel in Las Vegas in July of 1989, "It all began ten years ago with a man named Paul Bennewitz."[32]

Bennewitz was a business owner and physicist who began intercepting strange radio signals and snapping photos of strange objects over Kirtland Airforce Base and the Manzano Test Range in New Mexico in 1979. Bennewitz, who was unknowingly recording and photographing classified Air Force projects, came under secret observation from various intelligence agencies, including the Air Force's Office of Special Investigations. Doty was introduced to Bennewitz, and it was decided that the best way to deal with the situation was to begin convincing

[31] Jung, Carl. Flying Saucers. Routledge Classics. New York. 2002, xiv.

[32] Moore, William. *UFOs and the U.S. Government Part 1.* F ocus Magazine. Vol. 4, Issue 4-5-6. June 30, 1989, 4.

Bennewitz that the strange objects that he was seeing and recording were extraterrestrial in origin. The two men became friends, according to Doty, but part of the relationship hinged upon a lie. Over several years, Bennewitz became much more fixated on a theory, which he had worked out; a complex plot involving alien abductions and a potential invasion. His addiction to the story, and the complex collection of information and disinformation given to him by various people in the intelligence community, began to eat away at his mental health. Bennewitz, over the course of the 1980s, slowly unraveled at the seams.

The story of Paul Bennewitz is thoroughly explored in the book *Project Beta; The Story of Paul Bennewitz, National Security and the Creation of a Modern UFO Myth* by Greg Bishop. I will not spend much time discussing the events here, but, suffice it to say, when Doty and Bennewitz met, it would not be long before Doty's name would become infamous within UFO circles.

In an e-mail to Richard Doty, dated 30 November 2017, I asked him who he was and how he got involved in the world of UFOs. He explained that he attended the Air Force Office of Special Investigations (AFOSI) Academy in 1978. He was commissioned a "Special Agent" and assigned to the AFOSI at Kirtland Air Force Base in New Mexico. He worked in the Counterintelligence Division. According to Doty, his job was:

> ...to safeguard the Air Force priority resources located on base. I set up counterintelligence networks on and off base to report any threats against Air Force resources. My division created a "source" network around the base. This network would report any unusual activity outside the base perimeter that might be a threat against base resources. The network included retired military personnel who lived off base or close to the base perimeter. Civilians, who volunteered their services, and paid informants. We also recruited local news media personnel who would keep track of reports or stories about the Air Force base or Air Force personnel.

Doty explained that, in 1980, a UFO sighting occurred on the base, and he was tasked with investigating it. He writes:

> I conducted an intense investigation interviewing the witnesses and conducting an exhaustive follow up investigation. Part of the investigation was released based on a Freedom of Information Act

request. My name appeared in the report and thus I was introduced into the UFO community.

Doty retired from the AFOSI in 1988. He explained to me that he has often tried to put to rest the stories and mistruths concerning his work.

> I tried twice to explain my activities while in the AFOSI, regarding my investigations of UFOs. I was ridiculed, humiliated and rumors were spread that I was a disinformation officer for the US Government. I decided to just stay quiet and conduct my own business behind the scenes.

Doty has indeed suffered much from innuendo and rumour. Many in the UFO community view him as an enemy, a spook and a liar. To understand why, we must look at the history, and, indeed, the mythology, which surrounds him.

Doty's tale has been told and retold over and over again within the halls of UFO culture, and I do not wish to elaborate too much in this book. I care more about the man himself than the mysterious history that surrounds him. That being said, I will present a very brief history that highlights only a few key moments to provide some background.

The years between 1980 and 1989 were both surreal and absurd, and the chain of events led to the development of the longest lasting ufological mythology ever conceived, most of which is still discussed today within the UFO community, albeit most are ignorant of its source.

In 1980, UFO researcher William Moore co-authored *The Roswell Incident*: a book that was partially responsible for putting the small town in New Mexico on the ufological map. After a radio interview, Moore received a phone call at the radio station. He was contacted by a mysterious figure from the intelligence community who offered Moore a deal. In exchange for information regarding UFOs, Moore would potentially have to sew disinformation into the UFO community—in other words, to spread false information regarding the UFO phenomenon. He would also have to report back to various people in the intelligence world how that false information was being received. According to author Greg Bishop, Moore knew he was being used, but it was a risk he was willing to take. Moore gave this mysterious contact the name "Falcon."

In October of 1980, Falcon introduced Moore to Doty. He was to be Moore's direct contact in the intelligence community. As time went on, and as Moore's list of intelligence agents grew, Moore gave this little circle the nickname "The Aviary." Like some cheesy spy novel, every member was named after a bird.

~

There are a couple of theories as to who Falcon was. Greg Bishop presented a case for a high-level CIA operative and spymaster named Harry Rositzke. UFO researcher Brad Sparks guesses that it might have been Doty's superior officer, Air Force Colonel Barry Hennessey.[33] I decided to ask Doty about Falcon. In an e-mail dated December 8, 2017, Doty responded:

> Falcon was former CIA Director Richard Helms. That was proven several years ago. I met Mr. Helms in 1978. We became friends and were until the day he died. Mr. Helms was the man who knew the hidden secrets about the USG (United States Government) programs involving extraterrestrial contact. Mr. Helms knew the entire history and everything that the USG has done with, to and against the ETs since 1947. Mr. Helms was one of the MJ 12's up to the day he died on October 23, 2002.

I was surprised that a Director of the CIA would get involved in this whole UFO affair. Doty's suggestion that Helms was "Falcon" gave me significant pause. However, things were going to get much stranger.

Doty was providing UFO information to Moore and Bennewitz. In 1983, he would meet investigative journalist Linda Moulton Howe. She was invited to Kirtland Air Force Base and shown several classified documents by Doty. These documents provided details in regard to extraterrestrials, from the Zeta Reticuli star system, who were responsible for the genetic creation and evolution of the human race. Furthermore, the documents alleged that the aliens struck a deal with the United States government: in exchange for studying the alien technology, the American government was to allow the aliens to have free reign in mutilating cattle and abducting humans.

Absurd as it may sound, Howe bought the story and was told by Doty that she was being chosen by the American government to present this information to the public in some act of final disclosure of

---

[33] Carrion, James. Editor. *MUFON Symposium Proceedings 2007.*

the alien reality. Suffice it to say, Howe never received the files and the "truth" did not come out.

One year later, in 1984, a Hollywood producer by the name of Jamie Shandera, friend of William Moore, received a mysterious roll of undeveloped film. The series of photographs were pictures of documents that pertained to a flying saucer crash near Roswell, New Mexico in 1947. The documents pertained to a group of twelve military officials and scientists, code named Majestic 12, or "MJ-12," to ascertain how to harness the technology of crashed UFOs and the secrets behind the phenomenon. Moore and Shandera sat on these documents for three years, slowly collecting and receiving additional and updated MJ-12 files from secret sources. In June of 1987, the two men finally released the MJ-12 documents to the UFO community, convinced of their authenticity.

Turns out, the documents were total rubbish. Due to many errors within them, and after being subjected to expert examination, the general consensus was that the MJ-12 documents were good forgeries—either the work of the intelligence community as a disinformation campaign, or the fictional creation of a couple of opportunists attempting to make a name for themselves or even a quick buck. Furthermore, many members of the UFO community believe that Richard Doty was partially behind their creation. Doty explicitly denies this allegation.

Regardless, the MJ-12 documents became infamous. Significant aspects of the modern UFO narrative still stem from these papers. As with other stories in the UFO discourse, the fiction has become fact, and, if there is anything factual in the MJ-12 papers, they have become inseparable from the fiction. Whatever the case, the author or authors of these documents, whoever they may be, can proudly carry the mantle of not only shifting the subcultural narrative, but forming significant aspects of that narrative which are still entrenched within contemporary UFO debate.

On October 14, 1988, *UFO Cover Up?: Live!*, aired. This curious cultural gem, two hours in length, and filmed live, was intended to reveal all the secrets behind the UFO question. Hosted by Mike Farrell, of M*A*S*H fame, the exposé-style show contained interviews with ufology's best and brightest stars, as well as various witnesses, and high ranking military personnel. Jaime Shandera and William Moore were the star attraction because they had allegedly secured interviews for the show with two high ranking intelligence officials who could testify to the truth behind the UFO phenomenon; two members of the Aviary, Condor and, you guessed it, Falcon himself.

With voices masked and blacked out in silhouette, the two inform-
ants detailed a complex tail of crashed and retrieved flying saucers,
extraterrestrial biological entities (EBEs) found on site, and a lone
extraterrestrial survivor who would help the Americans establish
contact with its home planet. Fun fact: the surviving EBE enjoyed
Tibetan music and strawberry ice cream too.

While the show itself was utterly ridiculous, it muddied the waters
around Richard Doty. The synthetic electronic voice and black silhou-
etted Falcon was, at least to the broader UFO community, Richard Doty.

By 1988, Doty's name was attached to a lot of UFO (dis?)informa-
tion. In 1989, a UFO researcher from Colorado named Robert Hastings released a 13-page report. In it, he points the finger directly at
Doty. He writes:

> First, it has been established that "Falcon," one of the principle sources
> of the MJ-12 material, is Richard C. Doty, formerly attached to District
> 17 Air Force Office of Special Investigations (AFOSI) at Kirtland Air
> Force Base...[34]

Hastings goes on to state that he spoke with Linda Moulton-Howe who
says that when she met Doty in 1983, he identified himself as "Falcon."
He also explains that he met with a member of the production team
for *UFO Cover Up?: Live!* who stated that Condor was an Air Force
captain named Robert Collins, and Doty was 'Falcon.' Furthermore,
the segment in which Doty 'played' Falcon was pre-recorded. Moore
and Doty denied this at the time.[35] Doty strongly denies ever being recorded for the program. He asserts it was not he.

During the same year as *UFO Cover Up?: Live!*, Bennewitz completely fell apart. Convinced that not only was there an alien underground
base in Dulce, New Mexico, and that they were attempting slowly to
invade the planet via genetic manipulation programs, he was sure that
these aliens came every night and injected him with strange chemi-
cals. Barricading himself inside his home, and even arming himself,
he barely ate and slept. He was eventually checked into a hospital for
treatment. Paul Bennewitz died in 2003 at the age of 75. While his
death was totally unrelated to the deterioration of his mental health in

---

[34] Clarke. Jerome. *UFOs in the 1980's: The UFO Encyclopedia Volume 1.* Apogee
Books. Detroit. 1990, 104.

[35] Ibid, 105.

1988, he is curiously viewed today as a sort of martyr within the UFO subculture, a warning to other researchers and enthusiasts not to fall victim to intelligence men and acts of deception.

By 1989, Doty was the focus of significant attention, if not full-blown harassment, by the UFO community. Everything was drawn out into the open, however, at that year's MUFON Symposium held in Las Vegas when William Moore took the stage. As if drawn to be a perfect circle, or saucer, Moore disclosed his work with Doty, "Falcon," and other intelligence agencies to the UFO community.

Moore stated that Doty was not the original "Falcon." He explained:

> First of all, on the question of Richard Doty and "the Falcon," it is important to note that the name "Falcon" was invented by my partner Jaime Shandera and I [sic] in 1984 strictly as a way of facilitating our talking to each other about this person, particularly on the telephone, without having to use a name. Richard Doty, who continued to be liaison man, was similarly referred to by us as "the Sparrow." Neither "Sparrow" nor "Falcon" were aware that we were using these terms in reference to them, nor was anyone else to the best of my knowledge, prior to about mid-1985. It was in mid-1987, just after we went public with the MJ-12 papers, that at "Falcon's" suggestion and with the concurrence of Richard Doty, we began dropping subtle hints that "Falcon" might in fact be Doty. "Falcon" felt that such a ploy would be useful to him in continuing to protect his identity, while Doty, for his part, said that if anybody asked he could simply deny it and that would be that. We quite naturally agreed, and, as many of you are painfully aware, it turned out to be an excellent diversion—particularly with respect to the effect it had following the *UFO Cover-Up?: Live!* show, which was broadcast nationally in October 1988.[36]

Moore went on, concerning Doty:

> In all fairness to Mr. Doty, here, I should also like to comment that, in my assessment, Rick is much better at following the orders and implementing the schemes of others than he is at coming up with ideas of his own. Those of you who have devoted time and energy to constantly badgering this man for more information should be aware that all you are doing is making nuisances of yourself. Rick is

---

[36] Moore, 5.

not the man you're after—it's the person in the control position that's important here. As far as I'm aware, no one outside of my project has any idea who that person might be, or what his motives are.[37]

Moore continues by explaining his role in the Bennewitz case:

My role in the affair was largely that of a freelancer providing information on Paul's current thinking and activities. I had nothing whatsoever to do with the counterintelligence and the disinformation, although I either knew or was aware of a number of people directly involved with that end of things.[38]

I can only imagine the audience, a die-hard collection of UFO researchers, hearing these words. Paul Bennewitz, one of their own, driven to the point of mental collapse by his own government, all the while, another one of their own stood by and watched it all play out.

I want to jump ahead for a brief moment. Perhaps, in an attempt to shift some of the blame, Moore stated that:

As for Bennewitz, by 1981, he was gathering data from a variety of sources and amalgamating it with information being fed to him by a number of government people in whom, for some reason, he seemed to have an implicit and abiding faith. The story that emerged from this mélange of fact, fiction, fantasy, hearsay, hard data and government disinformation, was absolutely incredible! Yet somehow, Paul believed in it and set out on a one-man crusade to tell the world that malevolent aliens from space were in league with our government to take over the planet... Paul was his own worst enemy.[39]

Any faith the UFO community had in William Moore disappeared that day. The man who was partially responsible for putting the small town of Roswell on the map, sabotaged his ufological career. No one trusted him after that. Moore's "tell-all" stunt had an interesting effect: it brought to light many aspects of the story that were kept hidden, but it also destroyed him. After delivering the speech, Moore left the stage,

---

[37] Ibid.

[38] Ibid. pp. 6.

[39] Ibid.

rented a different hotel room from the one initially provided to him, and left Las Vegas shortly thereafter.

Perhaps Bennewitz was too trusting, easily duped, and, as Moore explained, would go off "half-cocked to virtually anyone who would listen."[40] However, it took two to tango in this case, and, regardless of Doty's e-mailed statement to me that the intelligence community did not spread disinformation within UFO circles, Bennewitz was a victim of such disinformation.

Moore claimed that Doty was one of the agents behind the Bennewitz deception:

> Richard Doty was one of these people; although I care to know Doty well enough to gain the impression that he was faithfully carrying out orders which he personally found distasteful. Perhaps it was for this reason that 'the Falcon' had chosen him as liaison person, although I really don't know. Frankly, I don't believe that Doty does either. In my opinion, he was simply a pawn in a much larger game, just as I was.[41]

I asked Doty about Bennewitz. He clearly stated that he was following orders, and the entire affair was to protect national security. Doty stated:

> The operational plan centered around determining what type of electronic equipment Paul had and just how was he tapping into classified communications systems on Kirtland AFB. Once we found out what he had, we then developed a plan to convince him he had tapped into ET communications and not classified US communications systems.[42]

Doty explained to me that all his operations followed a specific plan with objectives. What the UFO community refers to as disinformation, he and the intelligence world considers counterintelligence. Where these operational plans are? No one knows.

Excerpt from a Telephone conversation with UFO Researcher Paul Dean

---

[40] Ibid.

[41] Ibid.

[42] Personal correspondence. February 10, 2018.

MJ: "So what's your theory concerning Doty? I've been speaking to the man on and off now for a while. I feel like he is maybe misunderstood, or maybe he has no idea what is going on."

Paul: "Who knows? I've never been able to sort out the full story. No one has. If his actions are ever proven as officially sanctioned, I'm thinking it would be perfect from a cost versus result angle."

MJ: "What do you mean?"

Paul: "Well, if you look at the organisational structure of his office at Kirtland, like who he answered to and who he closely worked with, I've identified twelve people, one a Brigadier General no-less, who must have been knowledgeable of the forged documents, and his long-time focus on issues supposedly outside his jurisdiction. He was meddling in things while on the job, in other words. This tells me that maybe there was an official allowing his behaviour to continue. I mean, what better way to frustrate or confuse the civilian UFO community, if the Air Force so desired, than have him do it on an ad hoc, part time basis, with not much accountability. There is something else, too. Something I'm trying to dig into. In 2008, the CIA actually admitted to holding records on Doty, but nothing could be released because, to use their words, 'the material is properly classified.' That is pretty wild. The CIA would only have records on him if they had employed him at some stage, or if he was supplying them with information they could use. Or, maybe they were investigating him. Who knows? Maybe he was working for them in a disinformation role or is even now still on the payroll somehow. Maybe they pay him every once in a while, right? He makes a few comments on UFO stuff to stir the pot. Then they get guys like you and guys like me to focus on him, rather than doing more productive research. For a small investment, for the small amount of work he actually needs to do, they know the ripple effect will be significant. Big results for little work. Or, you know, he's just having fun. Screwing around with everyone for the attention. Who knows...?"

MJ: "I did ask him if he still gets paid by an intelligence organization. He said he was not able to talk about it. Told me that I shouldn't make insinuations as to what that means though. The conversation got stymied by... oh, he had this thing he told me once in a private message, something about an enigma, wrapped in a mystery and surrounded by a bunch of classified information. He's a really funny guy, a nice guy for sure. I'd buy him a beer if we ever met."

Paul: "Yeah. If he is still paid by the CIA, the question is why? What is he up to? What are *they* up to?"

~

The more I dug into Doty and his story, the more I was seeing conspiracy everywhere, even when there was none to be had. Was I staring too long into the abyss?

Dean eventually put me in touch with his colleague, Barry Greenwood, who has been looking into Doty for nearly three decades. Greenwood, being the rational archivist that he is, slapped me with some cold realism. I asked him his opinion on the whole Doty affair.

In an e-mail dated February 4, 2018, Greenwood wrote:

> Not a single piece of evidence has ever surfaced on Doty being given orders by his superiors on MJ-12, or of AFOSI ever conducting a decades long program of UFO fake news with Doty at the forefront. However, there is evidence that Doty was part of a fiction novel project on this very matter before MJ-12 ever became publicly popular, along with Bill Moore and Bob Pratt of the National Enquirer. With regard to Bennewitz, there was legitimate concern by the Air Force about him because he lived near Kirtland AFB and was openly reporting to them that he was intercepting strange signals on his radio equipment. If I was a base commander and a civilian near the base was picking up odd communications, I'd at least be concerned that he was listening in on possible classified base activity. It quickly became evident that Bennewitz was rather off the wall, and while the Air Force dropped the inquiry after one meeting with him, Doty, as a base OSI agent, did not, and pursued developing an odd relationship with Bennewitz involving Bill Moore. This is explained in a speech Moore gave in 1989 at a MUFON conference where Moore claimed he was an "unpaid government agent" working with Doty. Doty will tell you he has the truth, but he will never back it up with anything except his mouth and some very dubious paperwork.

If Greenwood was right, the entire story concerning Doty, his interactions with Bennewitz, Bill Moore and his associate Jaime Shandera, the MJ-12 documents, and the rest may have started as a counterintelligence operation, but very quickly became opportunist peddling to make a few dollars and enjoy a bit of fame. No one really knows.

Greenwood referred me to a series of documents known as "The Pratt Tapes," which were meeting notes and other documents by Bob Pratt with information regarding MJ-12 and Doty, dated between 1982 and 1984, several years before the MJ-12 documents were "leaked." At one point, at a meeting between Pratt and Moore, the documents refer to Doty as the hero of their novel, investigating UFO sightings, and getting involved with, and investigating, a Dr. Berkowitz (Bennewitz) who is convinced of an alien invasion plot, and a secret group of high level government officials who have been in contact with the aliens known as 'Majik 12.' The working title for the manuscript was originally "MA-JIK-12" but later renamed *The Aquarius Project*. The novel was never published and scrapped in early 1984. Greenwood, and another UFO researcher, Brad Sparks, who published a joint article in 2007, wrote that the novel had a third contributor, Ronald L. Davis, whom they believe to be Doty himself.[43]

When I presented this idea to Doty, he was not amused. Doty stated that he never met Bob Pratt of the National Enquirer, nor that he had anything to do with MJ-12 or a novel. He explained that there is no evidence that he was involved in any way. Doty put it to me bluntly, "anyone with some basic intelligence and common sense would understand I didn't author the documents."[44]

The Pratt Tapes are in no way a smoking gun. However, they do identify a recurring motif in Doty's ufological narrative: the constant interplay between fact and fiction, legitimate government documents and a writer's pen crafting the next big novel, a symbiosis of real and myth, permanently fused and impossible to disassociate.

The Doty I was speaking to on the telephone and through e-mail was a grandfather who loves his family; a man who enjoys a good glass of dark beer and German food; an overall nice guy as far as I could tell. The Doty I had been hearing and reading about was the man who played a role in shaping the UFO narrative of the 1980s: Doty the intelligence man; Doty the spook; Doty the disinformation agent. The two of them, the Doty I was interviewing and the Doty I was researching, had become one. By the end of it all, I struggled to tell the two apart. The Doty that Bennewitz knew was the same, a mix between real and false, a friend, but also an operative whose job it was to confuse and obfuscate.

---

[43] Carrion, James. Editor. "The Secret Pratt Tapes and the Origin of MJ-12." *MUFON Symposium Proceedings 2007*

[44] Personal Correspondence, February 10, 2018.

The more I got to know Doty, and the more I spoke to others about him, I knew I was dealing with what philosopher Jean Baudrillard called a *simulacrum*—where the artificial and the real become one, where the line between artifice and truth cease to exist. Furthermore, it was taking me down a path I did not want to be on: a path where I saw shadows in every corner.

Whatever Doty says will always be held in question by the UFO community, simply because history and mythology has made it so. What is not in question is the stark and brutal fact that someone was behind all this disinformation, this myth building. Whether it was Doty, or Moore, or someone in the Aviary, or someone else still cloaked in mystery, they are fundamentally responsible for much of our modern UFO lore. Even though much of the MJ-12 documents are known forgeries, even though there is no evidence to suggest that the government is in league with aliens, those myths continue to live on. The "evil" grays, "advanced aerial threats," and even alien implants, all stemmed from this decade, the 1980s, and much of it, by hook or by crook, was influenced by, or has influenced the perception of, one man—a Sergeant in the United States Air Force, Richard C. Doty.

The UFO community will continue to regard Doty as an "agent of disinformation," whether he deserves the title or not. They will also attempt, in vain, to sort out the fact from the fiction. Perhaps Doty was following his orders like a good soldier. Perhaps he was a pawn, as Moore suggests, in a larger game intended to destroy any credibility that the UFO discourse had with ridiculous claims of evil aliens and crashed flying saucers. Perhaps Doty, as UFO historian and archivist Paul Dean speculated, is still occasionally contracted out by the intelligence community to reengage with the UFO community, to stir the pot, and have focus placed upon himself instead of bigger ufological questions. His personal records with the CIA are supposedly still classified. Who knows, maybe he is still on the payroll. Perhaps he wasn't a disinformation agent at all, but is rather a 'long con,' not truly intended to provide disinformation but to *be* the disinformation, to be the boogey-man, the shadow, which generates anxiety within UFO circles. Perhaps he simply saw an opportunity to make some extra money, or just to mess with the people who believed in aliens and flying saucers. Or, perhaps, none of the stories about him are accurate. Perhaps he is simply a man who did his job, settled down with his family and is simply living his life, and the UFO community inflated his story to mythical proportions because that is its nature. Only one thing is true: at the end of the day, it does not matter.

Whether he likes it or not, his influence still exists today in the UFO subculture. As I explained to him once in a text message, his intent, whatever it was, no longer mattered. The only thing that matters now is the impact. Doty still has impact. You will often hear members of the UFO community referring to other researchers as "another Bennewitz" or even the use of the name as a verb, that is, one who is being "Bennewitz'd." This tale has become a cautionary one, as if it should only be uttered around camp fires in hushed tones, for, if you speak too loudly, old spirits will rise from the shadows. Doty's effect is as potent today as it was decades ago.

In my correspondence with Doty, perhaps the most interesting and compelling thing he wrote was the following. I asked him about his alleged role as "Falcon" in 1988 on *UFO Cover-Up?: Live!*

Doty's Response, 8 December 2017:

> *The UFO Cover-Up?: Live!* was on air in October 1988. I joined the New Mexico State Police in August 1988. I was attending the New Mexico State Police Academy from August through December 1988. I could not have possibly been on that show. I proved this several times, including an attendance roster presented in a court of law... I had 35 other cadets who could verify I was at the academy. The person on the UFO Cover-up might have been the "other" Rick Doty that so many within the UFO Community has created. I was supposedly on a Univision (Spanish language) TV program in 1991. Although I do speak fluent Spanish, I was not on any Spanish language program. I was accused of being on a British Talk Show in 1997; again, I was not. So, as you can see, someone else makes up a Rick Doty.

I was unsure what to think about this. A 'fake Doty?' At first, it did not make sense. I then realized that perhaps I was interpreting Doty much too literally. I realized that much like the UFO phenomenon itself, forcing logic upon an illogical phenomenon was a mistake. Perhaps, much like the ghostly UFOs he alleges to have seen, Doty himself is a ghost within the UFO subculture. His work with Moore, Bennewitz, and others within the UFO community, and his alleged involvement in various UFO documents, forged or altered, such as the infamous Weiztel letter, still haunt the UFO discourse. Doty's claim that there may have been an "other Rick Doty" is indeed more cultural than real, more philosophical than literal.

Carl Jung surmised that myth building "is the product of an unconscious archetype and is therefore a symbol which requires psychological interpretation."[45] Doty, as much as he is a man, is also a myth, a subcultural archetype. A trickster, or perhaps a shadow, he is a reflection of many cultural anxieties within the UFO community. His "identity" within the subculture is that of the specter, as discussed earlier in this book, and the UFO narrative flows through various mythologies that he has perhaps created, or, if he did not create them, then those that have been created about him.

Doty and I have had a strange relationship, and much of the time I've felt like a hen clucking about the fox's den. Doty has been kind and patient, and I'm sure that much of what he told me transgresses the normal boundaries between the realms of fact and fiction, but, as far as I know, he has never lied to me. No, perhaps he has lied, just once. Early on in our conversations, he told me, "I don't play the game anymore." Whether Doty knows it or not, that statement is not true.

Decades ago, Doty's actions shaped the UFO discourse and subculture. Those actions resonate now, no less potent than they were all those years ago. For the legends and mythos that surround Doty, time seems to be meaningless. More importantly, the subculture is haunted by those actions, still unaware of what exactly was real and what was fiction. Regardless of Doty's involvement in any of it, whether he was responsible or not, much of the UFO narrative bears his mark. Herein lies the anxiety: the fundamental unknown that lies in the gap of information and disinformation, that the opposition between truth and lie is incomprehensible. Doty as simulacrum, it no longer matters if he tells the truth or lies or tells a story that is somewhere in between: it is his specter, his *hyperreal and mythologized self*, which continues to haunt the subculture. It is not Doty the man, but what the subculture makes him out to be which is truly what matters.

With all this said, Doty's ghost begs one big and final question: who are the other ghosts haunting the UFO community who *create ideological truths* wherever they go? Is the UFO discourse, the narrative, made up totally of *ghost stories*? Perhaps the most frightening thing about Doty is not who he is or what he is purported to have done; perhaps it is that the UFO subculture sees itself in Richard Doty.

I stated earlier that Doty was an outsider to the UFO community. Perhaps I was wrong. Maybe he reflects it like a shadow, a dark mirror, sitting before it, and in the space between himself and the broader UFO subculture rests the gap where truth and lies intermingle and

---

[45] Jung, Carl. Flying Saucers. Routledge Classics. New York. 2002, 19.

where fact is a fugitive. In 1989, when William Moore told a packed Las Vegas ballroom that "It all began ten years ago with a man named Paul Bennewitz," he could not have been more wrong. Ghosts do not recognize the limitations of beginnings and endings. Moreover, we are also haunted by the ghost of Paul Bennewitz, a man who also played the game and now reminds the UFO community that there is significant peril from staring too deeply into that mirror. If Doty's specter is a grim reflection, and the UFO community sees itself there, then the story Moore alludes to has yet to begin. We are indeed haunted by ghosts, but we also become them when we attempt to spin our illusions as truths. Dare we enter the gap between realms?

Within that gap lies the stark awareness that everything we claim to know or understand concerning the UFO phenomenon is itself a lie, disinformation of our own design. It is an ideological prison of the ufological mind. Richard Doty is just a man. He is not someone we ought to fear or hate. While the ghost of Richard Doty, the archetype, the shadow, is what we need to concern ourselves with, the greater phantom is the UFO community itself.

CHAPTER 10

The Invisible College

Richard Doty is not the only ghost who has shaped, and still helps shape, the UFO community. In the book *The Invisible College*, Jacques Vallée presents the reality of a large group of individuals who quietly, and sometimes secretly, engage with the UFO discourse. Undoubtedly, invisible colleges exist worldwide in every human field of study and endeavour. Some of the earliest mentions of such organizations date back to the 17th century, found in texts and manuscripts which link to Rosicrucianism, a spiritual and cultural movement, which suggested that an alleged secret order existed to study various early scientific and spiritual phenomena. While undoubtedly fascinating, this book will only focus on the college as it relates to the UFO phenomenon.

In 2018, I interviewed Dr. Christopher "Kit" Green. He is a close friend of Vallée, and a public "member" of this group. According to Green, the invisible college is a virtual collection of men and women who remain in constant contact with their peers. They are driven by a curiosity, albeit a curiosity they are often not allowed to pursue publicly, in various anomalous and esoteric phenomena.

Somewhat similar to departments on a college campus, they typically gather at times to meet and hold private conferences where they share their ideas and work regarding the phenomenon. Many of the members maintain relatively high social or cultural status. They often possess advanced academic degrees and work in some of the world's top universities. Some own or maintain very high level professional positions in corporations and companies often associated with either technology or aerospace; some are individuals within government or the military, or are government contractors, and some have government clearance to access sensitive classified and top-secret information. While some have publicly stated that they have an interest in the subject, often to their own professional detriment, most remain hidden. No one knows exactly who they all are, nor do they necessarily know each other. Unlike the college campus model, this college exists in small collectives. Green, for example, has worked with the same dozen or so individuals for nearly forty years. While the invisible college reaches far beyond his specific circles, no one, Green included, is aware of every single member. Green consults with nearly sixty other medical doctors who share similar interests; however, they are not members of his specific collegial confederacy. Some of these collectives and confederacies know of others who engage in similar work, while some groups exist totally independently without the knowledge of any of the other collectives. The invisible college holds no roster of membership, no formal structure, and no formal leadership. In other words, there is no organization and no system. More accurately, the invisible college is a catch-all term for the existence of open-minded experts and academics who determinedly pursue the unpopular or esoteric questions and mysteries of our world, of which UFOs may or may not be a part, using their intellect, experience, connections and capital in that pursuit.

These individuals, both known and unknown, are simultaneously members of the UFO subculture and not. Much like UFO witnesses and experiencers, they straddle a gap between worlds. They are often insiders with access to sources of information within government, and in possession of significant academic and cultural capital. Simultaneously, they are outsiders because their professional peers would condemn them for participating in the fringe study of UFOs and other esoteric topics. Even more bizarre is that other members of the UFO community do not trust many within the invisible college, especially those who are public in their pursuits. The very access, which makes them insiders, also makes them outcasts.

In this chapter, I would like to present several members of this college. Each has their own interpretation of the collectives they form, and each has their own approach to how they entertain the UFO question. I must be clear that these individuals are merely the scratching of the college's surface. The vast majority of their confederates do not wish to have their names revealed, nor are they interested in any publicity whatsoever. That being said, I am less interested in the projects these men and women are working on, even though they are very fascinating. Instead, I wish to understand how they fit into the UFO subculture, and, more importantly, how their discourse and very existence affects the broader myths and narratives that surround the UFO phenomenon. Within the UFO subculture and within mainstream official culture, the invisible college is a collection of ghosts.

Dr. Christopher "Kit" Green is a name that many within the UFO community will recognize. In private medical practice in Detroit, Green also serves at the Wayne State University School of Medicine. He was a professor at the Detroit Medical Center and Harper University Hospital. As executive director of the Detroit Medical Center's Emergent Technology department, his work has undoubtedly revolutionized the medical profession. All this alone would serve as an impressive résumé, however, Green also served as an intelligence officer for the CIA. Working all over Europe, Green engaged with many other intelligence operatives running espionage and counterespionage primarily against the Soviet Union. Oddly enough, he and Richard Doty worked on a mission together, certain details of which are still classified. Green left the CIA in 1985, but is still an active consultant and advisor to various intelligence agencies. He was awarded the National Intelligence Medal and has since served on many governmental and academic committees and boards. Most recently, in 2016, he was asked to join an advisory board for the director of National Intelligence.

While Green's pedigree is undeniably complex, he is, at heart, a doctor who cares for his patients. I interviewed Green regarding his work and his thoughts on the UFO subculture. While the purpose of this book is the latter, I feel that Green's current UFO related venture does exemplify interesting aspects of the overall UFO community. His current medical project deals with individuals who have been injured by anomalous aerial phenomena. Starting in 2003, Green began to work with individuals who suffered injuries from unknown aerial objects. In 2007, offering treatment at no cost, Green has treated about 180 of these individuals. Green's selection criteria for his patients are not based upon simple anecdote. Each of his patients must undergo a rigorous screening process.

Green explains that each patient must witness and be physically affected by the anomaly within 50 meters. He was very clear to explain that these individuals were not suffering injuries from a significant distance, but at a very close range. The second criterion stipulates that all patients suffering from these injuries must have corroboration from a second witness who was present at the event. Third, all injuries suffered must be physical in nature. The vast majority of the cases involve mixed radiation burns, thermal injuries, and temporary and permanent hematological and neurological damage. Fourth, his patients must allow him to speak to their previous doctors and grant him access to their entire medical history. Fifth, they must undergo a battery of tests including DNA testing, endocrine and specialized blood tests and brain scans.

While he will accept anyone who can meet the criteria above, a large percentage of his patients are incredibly high functioning. A significant number of them have high level security clearance and some of them are active duty American special forces, intelligence officers, private government contractors, high level aerospace company employees, and military officers. Most of these patients have been referred to him by their superior officers. None of the individuals have been, or are engaged in, any sort of esoteric, paranormal or ufological culture; that is—and Green wanted me to make this very clear—they are not prone to flights of fancy or delusion nor are they UFO aficionados. While not all of his patients come from military backgrounds, his patients seem to be highly intelligent to the point of being savants in certain talents or skill sets and have no inclination to suggest that they had a paranormal or alien encounter. They are not UFO witnesses or experiencers who show up at paranormal conferences or give lectures claiming to be experts.

Nearly all of the cases involve the witnessing of small drone-like objects as well as medium to large metallic looking objects of various shapes. In rare cases, the objects witnessed resemble "orbs which are physical and moving in a purposeful manner." I asked Green specifically if any of his patients ever claimed to have had contact with entities or beings. He confirmed that about two to three percent of his patients have witnessed and been confronted by what he called "creatures." However, Green asserts that this is not evidence of anything alien or paranormal. There is evidence in his study that some of the patients may have suffered from visual and auditory hallucinations. The problem, Green points out, is that the numbers are just too small to be useful yet.

Geographically, these events are heterogeneous and occur worldwide. While Green could not be specific, he explained that most of the events concentrate on, near or adjacent to military bases, airfields and proving grounds. Many tend to be located in desert areas. He went on to say that the locations are often "classified desert locations like areas in Afghanistan, areas in Iraq, operational areas for special forces in Latin America, [and] Central America." He disclosed that about a dozen or so of his patients were injured on or near the infamous ranch in Utah, nicknamed Skinwalker Ranch. He went on to say that some of his patients were in or near highly secured areas such as Area 51, private aerospace testing grounds, and Special Forces training areas.

To Green, there is something particularly strange about the types of individuals who become his patients; Green refers to many of these individuals as being "supernormal" due to their intelligence, skills and abilities. This does not mean they are super human, like in the movies, but that they are savants in some way. I am reminded here by Vallée's assertion mentioned earlier from his book *The Invisible College*. Certain individuals who experience a UFO encounter have often developed a curious aptitude or skill, often related to psychic or mental processes. It is unclear if this is occurring with Green's patients; however, I mention it for the sake of posterity.

After her encounters, Amy's intuition seems to have shifted to a greater level of perception, often experiencing feelings of ill ease or dreams that tell of future events. I asked Green if he believed that the phenomenon was somehow attracted to certain people, perhaps via these "supernormal" traits, or maybe even through their genetics? Green, being a scientist, suggests that we need to be cautious. Currently, the evidence is still being collected. He explained that "the genetics may not, in any way, be necessarily related to the injury ideology." In other words, it may not be related to the individual, in that their special abilities or skills make them magnets for anomalous injuries related to unknown aerial phenomena; rather, due to these "savant like talents," they often end up working in careers or being given duties which place them in situations where anomalous activity occurs. In other words, it may be less about them and more about their current circumstance. Perhaps it is both, or neither. I must admit that trying to reason all this out without more data is all speculation.

The source of the injuries is, indeed, curious to him, and the patterns that form between the injuries and the individuals who suffer from them also seems to stand out. Green indicated that this does not mean that his patients are seeing alien spacecraft or monsters from some parallel dimension. He admitted that he could "better imagine that they were injured by human technology rather than shapeshifting aliens from Zeta Reticuli." Simply put, no physical evidence has presented itself that allows him to make the leap even to suggest that the source of these injuries is related to extraterrestrials or some otherworldly intelligence.

Regardless of the incidents themselves, Green's patients form an interesting category of individuals affected by the UFO phenomenon. Similar to Amy and the other witnesses I've spoken to, they exist in a nebulous ghostly realm. The physicality of their injuries is objectively real. They have burns on their bodies, strange anomalous blood disorders that manifested after their encounter, cuts and bruises, and other curious medical issues that can easily be diagnosed. The injuries are, for all intents and purposes, real. The sources of those injuries, according to mainstream cultural and scientific thinking, are objects of delusional minds and fantasy.

Previously, I mentioned the imaginal realm, what Corbin called the *mundus imaginalis*, as a place where our imaginations draw their source material. The imaginal, according to some scholars, is a place of very real and tangible things. It is a place filled with strange and bizarre forms, which are both physical, like this book in your hands, and non-physical like your dreams or nightmares. It is the in-between, the gap between our daily physical world, and the world of myths, monsters and ghosts. It is one of the few hypothesized places where a person can be physically and objectively injured by something that does not exist, or at least is not supposed to exist. Whether Green's patients were injured by some imaginal haunting or by secretive advanced human technology, they are another group who are dealing with our interpretation of the specter. They are trapped in a dualism, one that cannot be decided upon, and outside the paradigms of what we consider to be real and not real. Something harmed them, something that, according to our official and popular view of reality, does not exist.

One of Green's closest friends is another well-known figure within the UFO community. Dr. Hal Puthoff, a physicist who was involved in military research regarding psi in the 1970s, is now the chief scientist at the Institute of Advanced Studies in Austin, Texas. Puthoff manages a handful of other scientists in the research program, called EarthTech International, at the IAS. He still consults for the American military regarding top secret black projects, and his company holds several military and private contracts including Lockheed's Skunk Works, Department of Defence and NASA. His key project involves theoretical advanced propulsion systems, which can harness something called zero-point energy. Boiled down, ZPE is the lowest possible energy, which exists in quantum field theory as no particles exist there. Puthoff asserts that this quantum field of energy, which is constantly fluctuating, can be harnessed. In simple terms, he thinks it is the fabric which binds all the cosmos together. Once you can figure out how to draw energy out of it, your energy source is infinite and incredibly powerful. Many of his peers have openly called him a "crackpot."[46] I cannot comment on the validity of Puthoff's claim. I am not a scientist, so I have little knowledge on this subject. As a student of history and philosophy however, I am well aware that all giants in their respective fields have taken similar abuse. Only time will tell if smaller minds will scurry up his back to stand on his shoulders. Regardless of this theory, he seems to be called upon regularly to consult the military and aerospace industries regarding exotic physics.

He and Green often communicate regarding their UFO interests and have been confederates in this subject for decades. Puthoff and I spoke in the spring of 2018 and discussed his personal interpretation of this curious collective known as the invisible college. Puthoff reiterated much of Green's interpretation of how the college exists in a virtual community of confederacies but expanded upon three key ideas. First, he confirmed the connection that exists between these individuals within the college, and the communities of intelligence agencies, private contractors and corporations. Secondly, that information regarding the UFO phenomenon exists in a gap within culture. It is, in simple terms, something that the military and private industry has significant interest in, but, to broader mainstream culture, it is tabooed by the media. Finally, that the role of the broader UFO subculture ought to be to aid in reducing the stigma surrounding the phenomenon, and not making it worse.

To suggest that the UFO community can, at times, lean towards conspiratorial thinking is an understatement. Many within the community see shadows in every corner, and Puthoff himself has often been painted as a government "spook" and disinformation agent. Realistically, while he does have government clearance to top secret information, he explained that actually divulging any of that information would be

---

[46] Jacobson, Annie. *Phenomena: The Secret History of the U.S. Government's Investigations into Extrasensory Perception and Psychokinesis.* Backbay Books. New York. 2017, 390.

treasonous. When I asked him how the invisible college connected to the intelligence community, he stated that, at times, members of the various confederacies within the college do have clearance. He was very clear to state that classified information IS classified, and it was not discussed or divulged in any way. No college member, Puthoff included, wants to live in a jail cell. However, where this intelligence access does become useful is in being able to make contacts with individuals who work in other departments within the various government and intelligence branches and agencies. The government has a lot of data and information, which is both literally and figuratively everywhere. There is no single storehouse of data. No single access portal. As the old adage goes, the right hand does not always know what the left is doing; except you need to add a hundred few more hands.

Much of this data and information is not classified in any way. It simply exists in the ether of government files and server hard drives. According to Puthoff, finding people who know where to find that information is the essential useful connection. If certain information is classified, those connections can be used to help in having it declassified. It is not at all about leaking classified information, as that is illegal. Much of the work also involves finding buried information that is not classified and bringing it out into the light. Furthermore, much of the information is useless. Just because it exists in a government file does not mean that it is worth something. For every useful gem of data or information, there exist mountains of nonsense.

I asked Puthoff how private interests got involved, especially private corporations. Did they have a hand in this college? There is no doubt that high level corporate employees and even owners partake in the UFO discussion. Most famously, Robert Bigelow, owner of Bigelow Aerospace, has been actively involved in UFO and paranormal research. In May of 2017, Bigelow stated on *60 Minutes*, that he had spent millions upon millions of dollars investigating the UFO phenomenon and that he was convinced of an extraterrestrial presence visiting Earth. However, Bigelow is not the only aerospace and technology giant interested in the phenomenon. Both Green and Puthoff, as well as others I have spoken to who have chosen to remain anonymous, have been invited to attend private meetings and conferences held by various aerospace and technology companies. Acting in a consulting capacity, information and speculation regarding exotic technology and advanced propulsion is typically the sought-after treasure. What occurs at these meetings is a sharing of data, a kind of lending library where ideas move around.

The difference between the UFO community and the invisible college boils down to access. Being a member of a collective brings with it significant access to other individuals who either have government clearances, monetary capital, or access to research materials and resources, or a mix of all three. However, as Puthoff was clear to assert, it also comes with responsibility. Trust is essential. As both Green and Puthoff explained, their collective models the Chatham House Rule. The rule is simple:

> When a meeting, or part thereof, is held under the Chatham House Rule, participants are free to use the information received, but neither the identity nor the affiliation of the speaker(s), nor that of any other participant, may be revealed.[47]

After spending time with the UFO community, I can personally attest that this rule is not always followed. Not all confederacies within the invisible college are willing to work openly and publicly. They often view the broader UFO subculture as conspiratorial, paranoid, and smarmy. What ultimately occurs is that the UFO community often suffers from misinformation because its access to information is limited. Throw poor information into the mix with vainglorious "UFO experts" who claim to know the truth, and the result is clear.

Puthoff made it clear that there exists a disconnect between how the media portrays the UFO phenomenon and the actual interest which exists within government and various private industries. There is significant interest in the phenomenon from a military and technological standpoint. For some reason, however, the media and academic worlds do not agree with the former. There exists a stigma towards the phenomenon. The UFO taboo will be discussed in more detail later in the book, but, suffice it to say, it leaves the community trapped in a gap. The UFO community is not a collection of loons chasing something that does not exist—Puthoff himself says that UFOs very much do exist. Rather, the UFO community is on to something: something important. The problem is that *something* is unknown, and the broader UFO subculture has no clue what it is dealing with. At this point, there is only speculation.

From a more pragmatic standpoint, the academics and high-status individuals who constitute the invisible college keep a relatively

---

47 Chatham House Rule. https://www.chathamhouse.org/chatham-house-rule

low profile. Most do not show up on television news to be interviewed regarding UFOs, nor do they write books about them. They rarely, if ever, give lectures on the subject at UFO conferences. In other words, they stay out of the spotlight. If the media is hungry for a UFO story, all that is left to draw upon are the people who are all too interested in that spotlight. The problem is obvious. The attention-seeking supposed "experts" with a few scraps of information spin their message, and that becomes the meat of the UFO narrative.

The key players, then, in the UFO subculture and outside of it, are the skeptics. While not all confederacies that make up the invisible college are interested in bringing the UFO phenomenon more into the public domain (as many collectives are perfectly fine to work in their own little corner of the virtual world) there are many that are. Puthoff suggests that the skeptics are the ones who need to be convinced, at least partially. Critical thinkers tend to be the decision makers. If you can reduce the stigma enough that they want to pursue it, then they are the ones who can "move the ball forward." If the message continues to spread, and if the hypotheses and ideas become palatable, then more formal and official studies can be done to pursue answers to the UFO riddle.

I am reminded of a quote from the 2011 film *Moneyball* starring Brad Pitt. In a conversation with John Henry, owner of the Boston Red Sox, played by actor Arliss Howard, Pitt's character is told:

> I know you've taken it in the teeth out there, but the first guy through the wall—he always gets bloody. Always. It's the threat of not just the way of doing business, but in their minds, it's threatening the game. But really what it's threatening is their livelihoods. It's threatening their jobs. It's threatening the way that they do things. And every time that happens, whether it's the government or a way of doing business or whatever it is, the people who are holding the reins—have their hands on the switch—they go batshit crazy."

Reducing the stigma has cost many individuals within the invisible college dearly. Later, I will discuss Harvard professor John Mack who was secretly investigated by his university for academic dishonesty and ethics violations regarding his work with patients claiming abduction by aliens. The university concluded that Mack had done nothing wrong, and that he was a professor in good standing. However, it was the first time in Harvard's centuries old history that such an investigation had taken place, and Mack's life was turned upside down as a result. The primary reason for the investigation, which Mack himself called "Kafkaesque," was that Harvard had trouble in accepting a respected professor's entertaining a very "alien" idea. Puthoff himself told me that he knows many individuals in the college who have lost opportunities regarding grant money for unrelated projects, been removed from their positions in various professional and academic organizations and smeared by their colleagues for engaging with the "lunatic fringe." Isaac Koi, a pseudonym, is a fellow UFO researcher and colleague of mine who fears what would happen to his career as a lawyer if his ufological interests became public to his clients. Indeed, the first people who break down barriers truly get bloody.

That is not to say that any member of the UFO community spouting unsubstantiated nonsense is a legitimate boundary crosser and barrier breaker. From a personal standpoint, when someone states that they know what the source of the UFO phenomenon is, they must be handled with skepticism and care. As I've stated before, anyone who says they *know* what UFOs are is either delusional or trying to sell you something. In my interviews with Green regarding the anomalous objects and creatures, which his patients experienced, he put it quite bluntly:

> I have never received convincing medical data that has led me to believe that alien abductions were real. I don't know what they [UFOs] are. I don't know where they are from. But I don't have any reason to believe that they are from outer space or they are aliens, because I can much more easily find extremely advanced human technologies which have been worked on for 20, 30, 40 years. I don't have to invent aliens to explain what I see... I can better imagine that they were injured by human technology rather than shapeshifting aliens from Zeta Reticuli.

That is not to say that Green denies the possibility of something paranormal going on. Like any good scientist, he keeps an open mind; just not so open that everything spills out.

I was put in touch with one other individual who, it could be argued, is a member of the college. Dr. Gary Nolan is a world class immunologist and microbiologist at Stanford University. He runs Nolan Lab, a cutting-edge immunology lab, has written over 220 research articles, holds 20 American patents and is considered to be one of the best minds in the field. His interest in the UFO phenomenon is no secret.

He appeared in the 2013 documentary *Sirius* which, according to the documentary's subject, Dr. Steven Greer, postulated that the remains of a curious six-inch mummy found in the Atacama Desert in Chile was non-human. Nolan volunteered to run the genetic tests on the mummy. Much to the chagrin of Greer, the miniscule skeleton was a female baby who suffered from rare genetic mutations and most likely was stillborn, or died shortly after birth. In 2018, Nolan and his colleagues from the University of California in San Francisco published a peer reviewed paper in the journal *Genome Research* which highlights their findings.

The scientific paper, and the 2013 documentary, put Nolan on the ufological map. He also got in touch with Dr. Kit Green, mentioned earlier in this chapter, and the two have been working on a project together. Using a small and willing sample of Green's patients as well as other medically vetted individuals, the two have collected DNA samples from more than a few dozen individuals who allege to have had anomalous experiences. As Green put it, the subjects of the testing have "perceived aspects of the experiencer phenomenon." Presumably, this can range from alleged contact with strange objects, entities to other odd paranormal events. Nolan and Green are attempting to find genetic commonalities within the DNA of these individuals. The question Nolan wants to answer is whether some individuals have a fine tuned "antenna" for the paranormal. As of the date of this book's publication, the results have been sequenced and returned to Nolan. He and Green are now studying the results. This process could take years to complete.

Simultaneously, Nolan and Green have also taken MRI scans of their subjects and located, what they believe, to be a brain system that may correlate to their study. In late November of 2018, Nolan and Green presented their initial findings at the *Consortium for Space Genetics* at Harvard University. Their presentation, *"Can Genetic Differences in Intuition and Cognition Drive Success in Space?"* highlighted that certain individuals have increased connectivity between the caudate nuclease and the putamen. A densely connected caudate-putamen brain system, according to Nolan and Green, may be an indicator of high executive functioning, intuition, and IQ. While the findings are still in their very early stages, some have surmised that this hypermorphic trait may be responsible for a "sixth sense" which allows for precognition and other parapsychological effects. Moreover, some have even suggested that this brain system may explain why certain individuals have anomalous experiences such as contact with UFOs.[48]

Nolan admits that he can only speculate without the data, but he guesses that this genetic "antenna" is somehow related to intelligence. He explained that intelligence, and any trait or attribute, on a genetic level, can be made up of hundreds of genetic markers. The combinations of these markers are what make us who we are. He wonders if the data will prove that certain markers are over-represented in their sample population. He explained to me that his current hypothesis is that all humans have some genetic markers which work like an "antenna." For example, the odd feeling a person sometimes gets because they are being watched or sensing danger before it strikes. Certain individuals, what Green calls "supernormals," have a genetic predisposition, a collection of specific markers, which allow for a stronger "antenna." Nolan thinks that these individuals are often very perceptive, have high executive functioning, or are very intuitive. Nolan and Green are clear that this is not about people who claim to call aliens with their minds. Rather, it may be more akin to the psychological phenomenon of synesthesia, the curious intertwining of two senses, which are normally separate. For example, certain people may see a certain colour and immediately have an automatic olfactory response; in other words, they can "smell colour." Do people who claim to have had contact with non-human entities or other paranormal experiences function with a sort of 'sixth sense synesthesia?' Can someone interact with information, as Nolan explained to me, on some quantum level? Can they "see" or "hear" information outside of the regular five senses, data that can span great physical space or even time?

Nolan made it clear that this whole project is in its early stages. There are still a lot of questions. For example, is it totally possible to parse out individuals who had a dream, or a moment of delusion or fantasy versus those who had an authentic anomalous experience? It may be fair to ask if there is even a difference? Perhaps the world of fantasy, delusion and dreams is merely the other side of the reality coin? Is Corbin's *mundus imaginalis* simply a facet of reality that certain individuals have better access to due to their genetic make-up? Can some people better access a shared pool of humanity's collective consciousness? For

[48] Iandoli, James: "Is the Caudate-Putamen An Antenna for Anomalous Information?" Terra Obscura. < https://www.terraobscura.net/blog/is-the-caudate-putamen-an-antenna-for-anomalous-information>

the vast majority of our species' time on this planet, the world of my-thology, spirits and gods was closely tied to the world of the everyday. The separation of these "realities" is a relatively new phenomenon. Sha-mans have been around a lot longer than academic scientists. Keeping an open mind is essential, but so is waiting for the data to come in.

Nolan and Green's project, among others, form the basic build-ing blocks of the invisible college: quiet projects which take years of dedication and hard work. Nolan and Green will not have an an-swer tomorrow. They are academics and scientists; there is a sig-nificant process here, one which takes patience, time and money. When I asked Nolan who was funding this project, he explained that it was totally private money. While he wouldn't divulge who was investing in this particular project, he said that many simi-lar projects are funded by "lots of interested wealthy people in the world." More ghosts, it seems.

After speaking with Green, Puthoff and Nolan, I couldn't help but think that, much like Doty, it would not take much for anyone to fall into the rabbit hole of paranoia and conspiracy. Three men, two of whom have top secret clearance and are former intelligence operatives, and one, a world class expert in genetics, having conversations with me regarding their work on a topic with a history steeped in stories of cover-ups and deception. Strangely, I realized that I was dealing with ghosts. Much of the invisible college—primarily those who stay in the shadows—live dual lives: on the one hand, they are academics, govern-ment contractors, and employees who do their jobs and pursue their careers, and, on the other, they are attempting to chase down evidence or any scrap of useful information, which they can use to prove that our world is much more complicated than we ever thought. They live within reality, all the while attempting to subvert it.

It was odd that as I reached out to more people within the invis-ible college, the more began to reach out to me. Much like Amy and her UFO encounters, the more I pursued, the more who pursued me. Even my lovely (and ever patient) wife was questioning the validity of my evenings being spent chatting for hours on end with strangers who used to work for "this" agency or are professors at "that" university.

"Do you think that something is leading me down a path? Whatev-er this phenomenon is? Is it pushing me? Or am I just nuts, and this is all coincidence?" I asked my wife one evening: "I thought UFO people didn't believe in coincidence," she responded with a raised eyebrow and a knowing smile.

"Very funny."

I was either being haunted by something, or it was just a random series of events. Whatever it is, and whether there even is a path, I have been left with more questions than answers. I began to realize that this subculture was as confused as I was. The more time you spend looking, the more you learn how little you truly know. The real struggle is in understanding that to be the case.

Perhaps this is the point. Perhaps the invisible college, and, to some extent, the rest of the UFO community, is engaged in that struggle. There is no need for conspiracy because the conspirators have no additional information or answers; they are just as confused as everyone else. Instead, this phenomenon frees us. It enables us to look up into the sky and wonder: "What if?" We unshackle ourselves from the chains of conformity and assimilation by a society that limits our attempt to understand and question.

The UFO phenomenon/subculture is a reflection of ourselves, our fears and desires, our ghosts. In some curious way, *it*, whatever *it* is, tells us more about ourselves and the questions that we still have concerning our reality and our place within that reality. We are the phenomenon and it is we. We shape it as much as we are shaped by it. Mythology, any mythology, is simply a reflection of humanity. Beyond the obvious question regarding the objective reality behind a myth—in other words, is the phenomenon *real*?— we must look to how that mythology changes over time and how we reflect those changes. UFOs, aliens and paranormal phenomena may very well be manifesting into our daily reality, but the deeper question, and, indeed, the more important question, is how those stories shape us and how do we shape those stories? Does the UFO subculture act as a sort of beacon, and with every ping, the myth adjusts and morphs to fit our current paradigm and ideological framework? Is Nolan's antenna less about receiving a signal, and more about sending that signal out to whomever is listening?

I wish to conclude, here, with something Nolan told me during our interview. He said that while he still had significant questions regarding his "antenna" hypothesis, he explained that scientists typically "put out ideas as hypotheses that they probably already have confirmation about." He admitted that talking about this project publicly is to "pressure test" it before the findings come out, to begin easing the stigma surrounding the ideas, which the project may begin to challenge. Clearly, Nolan knew something that I didn't. Just before we ended the interview, he closed with something deeply personal. He said that we are "just a bunch of silly humans" who know next to nothing about how our reality works, never mind this strange phenomenon. He expressed that this whole undertaking "fills [him] with wonder" and that his "palette is more colourful" than ever before.

CHAPTER 11

Derrida and the UFO

In order to understand UFOs, then, we must inevitably study the community of people, which those UFOs affect, either directly, via experience, or indirectly, via discourse. It may very well be impossible to grasp the UFO enigma, as it simply may be too far beyond our scientific and social knowledge. Furthermore, the UFO as object, and all the strange and paranormal events that are associated with that object, is experienced only by people. The study of UFOs and the connected discourse must be combined with the study of the UFO subculture. Without people, the UFO, as object and symbol, does not exist.

Part 2 of this book will be a critical foray into the fabric of the UFO subculture. The purpose is not to provide a complete picture, as that is impossible for any subcultural examination. Subcultures adjust quickly, they adapt, and people shift between paradigms and ideologies rapidly and randomly, so a complete understanding in this case is not possible. Rather, it will be a treatise, which attempts best to frame the culture.

Before moving on, I want to note a fundamental connection between Amy's personal experiences, the other experiencers in Part 1, Roy, Richard Doty and the various individuals who form the invisible college, and that of the broader UFO community. We see repeatedly, even in UFO incidents and encounters beyond the scope of this book, a shifting of perception on the part of the witness and experiencer. Their perception of the world, the one they took for granted, is suddenly altered and adjusted. Something rears its head, a strange and complete

Other perhaps, and opens a doorway through which the imagination, and even the imaginal, seems to pour through. Even those within the UFO community, who have never witnessed or had a strange experience with the paranormal, also change in their perspective of the phenomenon. The more one engages with the discourse, the more they themselves begin to question the very nature of what we currently interpret to be real. Everyone in Part 1 of this book is a ghost, which drifts in and out of official mainstream culture.

The UFO community, the subculture, which ranges from the most overzealous ardent believer to the hardline knee-jerk skeptic and debunker, works not from a position of the status quo, but, simply due to the very nature of the conversation, from the gap between the real and the metaphysical. While the above statement may make sense for the true believers, it also applies to those who would argue that UFOs and the attached strange phenomena are nothing more than hoaxes and delusion. By the simple act of even debating over the existence of UFOs, the skeptical debunker only proves that the subject is something worth debating over. Nothing breathes life into something better than talking about it.

~

The UFO phenomenon has been identified as something which crosses, if not breaks down, boundaries. Witness testimony and the scant physical evidence that exists, suggest that this phenomenon defies gravity, physical laws, and even reality itself. It is something that is both amazingly and terrifyingly real, yet so unbelievable that it defies common sense. They are tricksters, a product of some imaginal realm, and technological objects, which can traverse vast distances. They are objective and subjective. UFOs both exist and do not exist.

I will rely in Part 2 on the work of the late twentieth century philosopher Jacques Derrida. The father of *deconstruction*, Derrida's work attempted to problematize the very nature of what we deem real, authentic, or objective. Though Derrida never explored the UFO question, his work can easily be applied here in a book about the UFO subculture.

When we look at the UFO phenomenon as a whole, from simple but curious lights in the sky to full blown encounters of high strangeness and abductions, we need to ask ourselves what do we mean by real or fact. If we tie something like "fact" to "Truth," then this all hinges upon a reality that we can completely understand or know in some objective sense. In other words, all mysteries are solvable and knowing all things is possible. Derrida points out that this complete understanding of an objective reality is essentially impossible. For Derrida, while an objective reality does exist, it is inaccessible. All knowledge stems from language, as one cannot communicate ideas outside of it. *Differance* (with an 'a') is the Derridean idea that language and communication differ and defer from the actual objective thing the words are trying to explain or communicate. We cannot communicate about the real because the words and symbols that we use to try and describe it, constantly add layers of unreal information.

I will begin with the idea of language as something which defers. Say I am telling you about a UFO. I say something like, "The UFO..." and then add "...was hovering over the Statue of Liberty..." followed by "...in New York City." I then say, "...It was silver and round." As I continue to add information, the meaning of the original, "The UFO..." changes in your mind. Imagine, instead, as I was saying, "The UFO..." I was cut off because my mobile phone began to ring and I was unable to tell you about the hovering, the Statue of Liberty, New York and that it was silver and round. The meaning of UFO would have been different from what it would be had I been able to provide the fuller explanation. Simply, the more information I tell you, the more the meaning is revised and changed. Our access to meaning, to Truth, is deferred due to language.

Language also differs. Derrida posits that a word's meaning does not rest in some mysterious relationship between itself and the actual thing in the world. Rather, the word takes its meaning from its place in the entire system of language. When I say the word, "UFO," the word has meaning because it differs from other words, like "automobile," "helicopter," and "cloud."

Derrida basically points out that language is not a clear-cut system. First, the meaning of anything that we communicate is essentially deferred because it depends on what else we say. The meaning of that, in turn, depends on what else is said later. This will essentially go on ad infinitum: deference built upon deference. Secondly, the meaning of any term that we communicate is built upon the terms, which we do not use. Language, communication and knowledge itself is not objective, then, but rather, always changing and shifting. Truth, and what we deem to be factual or real, is problematized by Derrida's philosophy. If meaning is something that can always be built upon or stripped away, then all that we take for granted to be true is essentially both factual and fictional.

Derrida's linguistic theory complicates everything. Science, both as a process and the benchmark of an academic community, views itself as being objectively factual. Many scientifically minded people will undoubtedly recoil in disgust but science itself is subject to *différance* just as language is. Does not all science base itself upon the use of language and human communication? Are not scientists mere mortals like the rest of us who approach reality with cultural and social backgrounds, values, and ideologies? Boo. Hiss. Moreover, humanity's entire assumed system of governance and politics, economics, value and belief systems, race and gender politics—everything we deem to form consensus reality or common sense—is also subject to Derrida's hypothesis. Even Derrida's hypothesis itself exists within... itself. To put it bluntly, absolutely nothing ought or can be taken for granted. It is not that objective reality does not exist: it does, but it's just as slippery as hell.

UFOs naturally fit into this model. UFOs, simply put, are both fact and fiction simultaneously. Their objectivity and authenticity are in a constant state of duality, shifting in and out of cultural and social frames of reference. They do not attach themselves completely to a reality, which we currently understand; therefore, to make claims of "Truth" about them is impossible. This very dualism is touched on by two of Derrida's philosophical constructs: the undecidable and the ghost.

Both concepts were born out of a similar inherent problem, which Derrida saw. He suggested that many cultural ideologies exist in an "undecidable"[49] state. An *undecidable* is that which cannot conform to a side of a dualism—something that can be both fact and fiction, or subjective and objective, or present and absent simultaneously. His purpose was to shift our perception of common binaries that we use in daily life, such as male versus female or black versus white. Derrida saw that these binaries were not truly separate from each other; rather, they *differed*, and formed a more complex symbiotic state. For example, the very notion of being 'male' comes from aspects, comparisons and contrasts to being female. The two are not diametrically separate or different because they *require the other to define themselves*; in this duality, they form one construct where meaning and meaninglessness exist. Philosopher Claire Gorman explains that an undecidability "is the bleeding of boundaries..." where "binaries are dismantled" and meaning itself is altered. Here, in this process of crossing borders, our

---

49. Reynolds. Jack. "Jacques Derrida." *The Internet Encyclopedia of Philosophy.* http://www.iep.utm.edu/derrida/#H5

assumptions and paradigms change. What we end up with are "new perspectives and interpretations."[50] To put it in another way, Derrida asks us to cease viewing the world in structured absolute binaries because those absolutes require the other to exist. More importantly, as Gorman points out, when we move beyond these binaries, we gain new insight into our world.

However, just because something is undecidable does not mean that one cannot come to a decision regarding its state. The decision, which one makes as to its state, however, is not grounded in knowledge or some objective *Truth*, but in its *différance*. The decision often is made out of our preconceived values, social paradigms or ideologies. It is a culturally or socially based gut decision that "feels" right, perhaps due to media influence or public consensus, rather than being objectively or universally "true." Cultural and social paradigms remain in states of flux, often reflective of current paradigms. Subcultures and communities are also consistently in this state of constant change. The everyday world that we engage with is not a stable constant, and neither are our ideas, beliefs and knowledge. Rather, we are all dislocated and disjointed. We are haunted by ghosts, which call upon us to recognize that our assumed social world is nothing more than a shadow.

Early on in his work, a common undecidable that Derrida often spoke of, was that of the ghost—the specter which is present and absent, alive and dead. Later in his career, Derrida formulated that the ghost was the penultimate undecidable, impenetrable to deconstruction or any interpretation that wasn't rooted in ideological fallacy. In other words, one could not *feel out* its side of the dualism. Deciding whether a ghost is real or not real is impossible, as it exists in both of those states at the same time. Derrida suggests that the ghost is "an elusive specter [that] engineers a habitation without proper inhabiting." It is "virtual" and "a simulacrum" yet, in its very repetition of appearance to an observer, in its "haunting," it exists not only in memory or the mind, but as something real which motivates action in our physical *real* world.[51]

However, even with its continued appearance and reappearance, it is impossible ontologically to know the ghost; it is both real and not real, present and absent. As Derrida suggests, using the famous line from Shakespeare's *Hamlet* as an example, it is impossible to "comprehend

---

[50] Gorman, Claire. *The Undecidable: Jaqcues Derrida and Paul Howard*. Cambridge Scholars Publishing. 2015, 3.

[51] Derrida, Jacques. *Specters of Marx*. Routledge: New York. 1993, 6, 20.

the opposition between *to be* and *not to be*."[52] Ghosts haunt, and they muddy the water between fact and fiction. Derrida borrows another line from *Hamlet,* suggesting that ghosts epitomize the unknowability because, to and for them, "time is out of joint." It is not that ghosts haunt at a certain time, rather, they are continuously present in our minds, and, at times, physically reminding us of their presence. Derrida notes that a haunting occurs when the ghost "begins by coming back." While, as a noun, a haunt is where the specter resides, albeit not all the time as they come and go, as an adjective, to be haunted denotes a constant state of movement. When one is haunted by their ghosts, those ghosts not only come and go, but they are timeless. Location and time is meaningless to the ghost, and this imbalance also creates imbalance in the one being haunted.

Literary scholar Elisabeth Loevlie explains: "To live is to be haunted. Our 'here and now,' our material presence, is never stripped, bare or alone. Neither is our subjectivity. We are always caught up in invisible and intangible webs of the past, of the Other, of the future, of death. Our existence is therefore always in-between, defined of course by the materiality of our present being, but also by this immaterial flux that surrounds and situates us."[53]

We are, in essence, shaped by our ghosts. We leave one foot in our material world, our daily life where we go to work, pick up our kids from school, and watch television. We also leave one foot in another world, where our minds, both individual and collective, are defined by our pasts, our societies, our futures, our dreams, and our fears. A world where our ideologies and thoughts create the ideas, which make us who we are. The ultimate question that we must ask ourselves is, what resides in the gap we straddle? The middle ground between our worlds, the gap, the in-between, is where we find ourselves, in this realm of ghosts.

Interestingly, *the ghost*, and its predecessor, *the undecidable*, is that, much like a trickster and Corbin's *mundis imaginalis*, the concept itself remains open to further shifts in interpretation, to *différance*. We can read the ghost in a certain way, but, due to its ability to cross boundaries and realms, our reading must also shift with it, and ultimately it

---

[52] Ibid.

[53] Loevlie, Elisabeth M. "Faith in the Ghosts of Literature. Poetic Hauntology in Derrida, Blanchot and Morrison's Beloved." *Religions Journal. Issue 4.* July 4, 2013, 336-350.

will. It is unstable and transient, and so, too, is any meaning or truth that we attempt to derive from it. The ghost is not something, which we attempt to understand, as that is impossible. Rather, it is something that we maintain an awareness of: what Derrida once called "the heart of the living present,"[54] that which we engage with at the moment with no hope of trying to sort out an objective meaning.

To be clear, in his book *Specters of Marx*, Derrida was not directly speaking to a belief in ghosts as spirits of the dead, or as some supernatural force. His interest was not in the paranormal at all. Specifically, Derrida's project aimed to call into question the social and cultural ideas that were taken for granted in post-Cold War Europe with the collapse of Communism. In a broader sense, Derrida postulated that the social norms and paradigms of our daily lives are an illusion, a cultural and ideological ghost, motivated by both fact, such as historical events, and fiction, such as mythologies and social constructs, simultaneously. We are haunted by this ghost; it has no time or place, but it governs our perception of what we deem to be real. As philosopher Fredric Jameson put it, "...the living present is scarcely as self-sufficient as it claims to be; that we would do well not to count on its density and solidity, which might under exceptional circumstances betray us."[55]

In other words, the world that we've built for ourselves, what we refer to often as consensus reality, mainstream culture, or official culture, is not set in stone. Our cultural and social reality, the world we live in, the rules and boundaries set by science and language, exist (and do not exist) in a constant state of change. Literary scholar Colin Davis writes that the Derridean ghost is "a wholly irrecuperable intrusion in our world." His point, which encapsulates how I wish to use the idea of the ghost in Part 2 of this book, is that as we move about our daily lives, we are haunted. The ghost manifests in strange ways "which is not comprehensible within our available intellectual frameworks, but whose otherness we are responsible for preserving."[56] In other words, the ghost enters into our collective normal everyday world, incomprehensible

---

54 Derrida, Jacques. "Echographies of Television: Filmed Interviews." 2002, 131.

55 Jameson, Fredric. 'Marx's Purloined Letter', in *Ghostly Demarcations*, 26–67

56 Davis, Colin. "Hauntology, Specters and Phantoms." *French Studies.* Volume 59, Issue 3, 1 July 2005, 373–379. Found online at: https://doi.org/10.1093/fs/kni143

and unknowable, and shows us that our actions, decisions, thoughts and realities are merely shades and illusions, which are formed by objective events in our environments, and the many myths, ideologies and ghosts that haunt us.

Returning back to UFOs, they, as objects and experiences, are both present and absent, and, culturally, they both exist and do not exist at the same time. The UFO itself is a ghost, something which manifests and haunts not only an observer, but all culture itself. Moreover, the UFO community is a ghost, or perhaps a vast chorus of ghosts, who challenge the various underpinnings of the social world that we take for granted. In other words, mainstream and official culture, our contemporary set of ideologies, become meaningless before the phantom.

Moving into Part 2 of this book is to move beyond experience into theory. The UFO is not only an object, but a complex web of cultural lore intermixed with the ideologies and paradigms of the people who experience them. They are, in simple terms, stories, and, as author Julian Wolfreys explains, "To tell a story is always to invoke ghosts, to open a space through which something other returns... all stories are, more or less, ghost stories."[57]

We must then conclude that UFOs, as much as they affect the observer and the experiencer, also affect the entire subculture and broader mainstream culture. Those stories create a reality, and that reality forms the foundation of what we call the UFO subculture.

---

[57] Wolfreys, Julian. "Victorian Hauntings: Spectrality, Gothic, the Uncanny, and Literature." New York: Palgrave. 2002, 3.

PART 2:

FROM SUBCULTURE TO EXOCULTURE: A TREATISE ON THE UFO SUBCULTURE

"You and I both know that the house is haunted,
Yeah you and I both know that the ghost is me.
You used to walk around screaming, all slamming all 'dem doors.
Well I'm all grown up now and I don't scare easy no more."

—ALEJANDRO ROSE GARCIA AND ESME PATTERSON
FROM THE SONG "DEARLY DEPARTED."

CHAPTER 12

A Brief History of
The Phenomenon

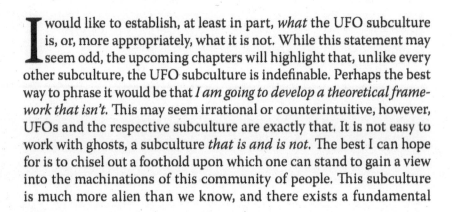

I would like to establish, at least in part, *what* the UFO subculture is, or, more appropriately, what it is not. While this statement may seem odd, the upcoming chapters will highlight that, unlike every other subculture, the UFO subculture is indefinable. Perhaps the best way to phrase it would be that *I am going to develop a theoretical framework that isn't.* This may seem irrational or counterintuitive, however, UFOs and the respective subculture are exactly that. It is not easy to work with ghosts, a subculture *that is and is not.* The best I can hope for is to chisel out a foothold upon which one can stand to gain a view into the machinations of this community of people. This subculture is much more alien than we know, and there exists a fundamental symbiosis between the people who make up the UFO community and the unknown phenomenon which engages with that community.

I would also like to be clear that, in the coming chapters, I use the term *extraterrestrial* as a catch-all term for *the non-human Other* (at least in the way that we typically mean human). Within UFO circles, the term typically refers to flesh and blood beings, aliens, who exhibit often human tendencies and emotions, as portrayed in film and television. To suggest that the UFO phenomenon is the product of such beings is an assumption based upon speculation. Maybe the phenomenon is truly caused by flesh and blood beings from another planet; however, within the UFO subculture, this is merely one hypothesis. It could very well be something else. For all we know, it could be some bizarre communal psychological manifestation. It could be entities from some other dimension who ride humanity's collective consciousness like a wave. It could be some other powerful universal force yet unknown to our collective lexicon. It could be all of those things at the same time. It could be anything. For the purpose of this book, I use the term *extraterrestrial*, but make no assumptions as to what the source behind the UFO phenomenon is. That being said, the UFO subculture has been chained, at least within popular media and culture, to the more mainstream literal, and material, interpretation of the alien. More on this shortly.

This symbiotic relationship forms the base of the framework, a collection of history, mythology and ideology that, on a cultural level, creates a subculture that supersedes culture itself. It not only opposes mainstream and official culture, but it also creates its own reality where the status quo is not allowed to exist. While we may perceive that the UFO subculture exists upon the cultural edge, or the fringe, its true place, much like UFOs themselves, is nowhere and everywhere. In other words, the UFO subculture is not a subculture at all, but something totally and fundamentally alien.

The following is best regarded as a treatise on the UFO subculture. I will begin by highlighting the historical and mythological origins of the UFO phenomenon. From there, I will present the case that the UFO community is a culture of outsiders; that the identity of the community is that of Otherness and that it has been ostracized from mainstream power systems, such as scientific academia, due to two reasons. First, due to its alleged ties to the construct of the extraterrestrial, which calls into question the rule of those power systems. Secondly, and more importantly, that the UFO community itself not only functions outside of those power systems but also calls their validity into question. Lastly, I will propose that the UFO subculture exists so far outside of the mainstream cultural boundaries that it erases those boundary lines altogether. To put it another way, the UFO community has been alienated to the point that it alienates the popular. The UFO subculture is not a subculture at all but alters our very understanding of how culture functions and exists.

To begin, one must address the history, which played a role in its creation—a ghost from the past, which still haunts us today. To do this, we must begin with a simple overview of the events, which led to the creation of what we understand today to be the UFO subculture. Consider the following to be a brief foray into an abridged ufological history.

As cultural theorists know, however, history is only one factor in how a subculture forms. History does not occur outside of culture, and the social and cultural paradigms and mythologies also play a significant role in the narratives that shape the subculture. Therefore, all subcultures are not only products of their history, but also of the broader social and cultural landscape in which they dwell. They are of two worlds, the events themselves and the ideas, thoughts, and social constructs which lead to those events and/or arise out of them as a result. The UFO subculture is a product of this duality, this symbiosis, this objective/subjective state, which is based upon historical events, but also the cultural and social spirits, which haunt *around* those events.

Are extraterrestrials visiting us? This is a fundamental ideological question which plagues, yet maintains, the UFO subculture. It is strangely essential to UFO discourse. While mainstream culture and science consider this idea absurd, (at least in any serious conversation) it is the glue which holds the study of UFOs together. UFO researcher Lorin Cutts writes that:

> Many now associate the UFO term exclusively with the subject of extraterrestrial contact. Thanks to frivolous media and a potent cultural pairing of expectation and imagination, the UFO acronym has largely changed from meaning *Unidentified Flying Object* into what we simply wanted and expected UFOs to be.[58]

---

[58] Graham, Robbie (ed), *UFOs: Reframing the Debate*, White Crow Books, 2017, 82.

Many within the UFO subculture suggest that they have a mountain of evidence proving that an *intelligent Other* is visiting Earth. This may very well be true. However, it is not the evidence which matters, at least for the purpose of this book, but why that evidence is not taken seriously by anyone else. Furthermore, we must begin to explore the connections between the history of the UFO phenomenon and the UFO subculture itself. How did this relationship between extraterrestrial and culture form, and the begged question: how does this relationship affect the subculture?

There is a small handful of people within the UFO community who dedicate their ufological work to archiving and historical research. Paul Dean is one of the most well respected historical minds and archivists in the UFO community today. In our conversations, he informed me that archivists are a subculture within the subculture, and perhaps only a dozen or so are still doing this type of research and work. He reached out to his colleague Barry Greenwood, whose name, for anyone involved in regular UFO research, carries significant gravitas. I asked them a simple question. From a historical standpoint, how did UFOs come to be intertwined with the concept of extraterrestrial visitation? Assuming that a fun Friday night for UFO archivists is mulling over UFO history, the two simply decided to write a short joint essay, which will be published for the first time in the appendix of this book. Their essay will be quoted thoroughly in this chapter. Dean informed me that, for the purpose of this book, they simplified the historical information as much as they could.

I recall in one of our video chats, Dean said, "How much do you want us to write? We could probably do twelve."

"Twelve hundred words. Yeah, that's perfect."

"Hundred? I meant thousand!" Paul Dean is never short on words.

We settled on roughly three thousand, and Paul Dean did not take the disappointment well.

It is generally accepted among many within the UFO community that people have been witnessing odd things in the sky for thousands of years. Our ancient ancestors recorded many odd atmospheric phenomena. As Greenwood and Dean point out:

> Reports of "flying shields," "flying ships," and "flying torches" can be found in Roman literature, baffling witnesses who noted such details within their minds' eye and context of the time. Later, "flying wash basins," strange dark globes in the sky and bodies crossing in front of

the sun had been reported in the middle ages. Odd bodies in the sky can be found in paintings and broadsheets during the 15th and 16th centuries, notable examples being a 16th-century woodcut by Samuel Coccius (Samuel Koch) and Samuel Apiarius, a September 1609 report from the then Kingdom of Joseon in present day South Korea of a flying "bowl" that maneuvered in the sky, attempted to land, and took off again in a shower of sparks, and the 1486 painting 'Annunciation with Saint Emidus' by Carlo Crivelli of a miraculous halo.

Odd events indeed, but, for obvious reasons, these events are generally chalked up to being "interesting" but cannot be used as hard material evidence of anything particularly alien. One cannot investigate a centuries old sighting, and, while the ancients did have good insight into atmospheric events and astronomy, humanity has gained significant knowledge since. We must not discount these events outright, but we must also be cautious of reading too much into ancient reports of anomalous activity.

Tales of beings from outer space have been around for a long time, but the last one hundred years or so have really established this as a cultural construct. Greenwood and Dean write that:

> The rise of human aviation and increasing interest in the sky and beyond led to accelerating the rise of a genre of literature, science fiction, which can be seen becoming popular in the works of Jules Verne and early writers influenced by the industrial and scientific revolutions which had been ongoing for some time.

Verne's famous airships made such a literary and cultural impact that it did not take long for the fiction to be interpreted as reality. Greenwood and Dean refer to an event in November 1896:

> Residents of northern California reported seeing strange aerial vehicles, airships, in the first large wave of reports of apparent unidentified flying objects. There was much speculation as to the origin of the airships, most revolving around the activities of mysterious inventors. Yet some wondered if there was another, more exotic, explanation.

While the newspapers of the day sensationalized the story, Greenwood and Dean point to one particular headline, "Mars and Venus Under Suspicion" in the San Francisco Chronicle from November 25th, 1896:

This suggested mistaken observations of Mars and Venus in the sky could have accounted for reports, but a quick reading of headlines like this can be read as suggesting other planets were in the mix of discussion.

Another newspaper in their archive, the Stockton California Daily Mail from November 19th, 1896, stated that a Colonel H.G. Shaw encountered beings from Mars while investigating a mysterious airship. According to Greenwood and Dean:

Mars was the object of much speculation as being the home of an intelligent civilization. Percival Lowell just a few years earlier had published a book about canals on Mars being the product of intelligence (Mars, 1895). So one can see the beginnings of connecting the mass reporting of sightings of mysterious aerial objects with the activities of beings from other worlds.

However, we must look beyond historical events, and explore how the scientific world, well established in the late nineteenth century, was engaged in a war for ideological control. After Charles Darwin published his theories on evolution in 1859, a movement based upon occult and spiritual principles began to take root in the minds of the British and American public. Founded by Helena Petrovna Blavatsky, Theosophy became very well established by the early 1890s. It was a direct challenge to the scientific work concerning human evolution and attempted to tie together aspects of science with the divine. In simple terms, it imposed a sense of mystical order upon the chaotic universe.

The root of Theosophy comes from Blavatsky and her alleged communication with a group known as the Ascended Masters, usually reincarnated monks or other similarly enlightened beings, who would provide her with messages to be recorded. As anthropologist Christopher Roth points out,

Most of the vocabulary of the New Age—auras, astral projection, chakras, spirit guides, gurus, the Age of Aquarius—can be traced directly to Theosophical writers.[59]

---

[59] Roth, Christopher. "Ufology as Anthropology: Race, Extraterrestrials, and the Occult." From E.T. Culture: Anthropology in Outerspaces. Ed. Debbora Battaglia. Duke University Press. 2005, 45.

Much of Theosophy drew from Eastern religious ideology, including some interesting theories as to the source of the human race. Blavatsky established a very complex mythology of racial origins. Today, only handfuls of practitioners and occult researchers retain an orthodox view of classical Theosophy. To most, the vast majority of her writings are not only considered nonsensical, historically and geographically inaccurate, but also, at times, racist. Contemporary New Age spirituality, the modern product of Blavatsky's work, has significantly softened, if not done away with, some of the more prejudicial and racial overtones of its original source material. That being said, Theosophy did establish a certain ideological paradigm in its day in that humanity was aided by enlightened extraterrestrials from the planet Venus. Not only did they supposedly aid in human evolution, they also constructed the Pyramids and ensured that secret organizations, such as the Freemasons, would pass along this secret knowledge from generation to generation.[60] As Roth points out:

> Each of these scenarios emerges again in standard scenarios in ufology and in the subdiscipline of "ancient astronaut" historiography.[61]

Even though Theosophy's popularity began to dwindle, leading up to the First World War, its influence had spread. The image and ideas concerning benevolent men from Venus had taken root and provided significant source material for UFO discourse in the future. During that same time, H.G. Wells' *War of the Worlds* published in 1898 would have enriched the extraterrestrial mythology and influenced social consciousness towards a possible extraterrestrial reality for modern Western society. Furthermore, Wells made an interesting technological addition, which put a twist on the extraterrestrial narrative. Wells did not depict well-meaning and quaint aliens with fanciful, albeit simple, tools; his aliens were here to invade and possessed significantly more powerful and terrifying technology.

Today, this conflict of messaging still exists within UFO discourse, and has spilled over into the politics of the UFO community. Much time is spent in debating, not whether aliens are here, but, instead, what are their intentions? Do they come in peace or are they a threat? This dual nature of the extraterrestrial can find its source in the late

---

[60] Ibid, 46.

[61] Ibid.

19th century but remains a discursive outlier in early UFO discourse. It isn't until much later that this good versus evil alien mythology becomes a common ufological paradigm.

Sightings of strange objects continued into the 20th century. As humanity's technology continued to develop, and for the first time in history, our species, under the genius of the Wright brothers, developed the ability to fly in heavier than air machinery. Thus, the genre of science fiction became increasingly popular. Technology, modern technology, was changing, and quickly.

With the popularization of radio, Greenwood and Dean point to another event, which may have shaped the public's perception regarding the extraterrestrial construct. On October 30th, 1938, Orson Welles broadcast his famous adaptation of *The War of the Worlds*. Greenwood and Dean write:

> Merely hearing talk on the radio of a Martian invasion, though fictional, was enough to throw thousands of inattentive listeners into a panic, believing it actually happened. Science fiction was no longer ridiculous speculation to people but was becoming a potential peek into the future.

We can view all this as the proverbial "priming of the pump." While the concept of the technologically superior extraterrestrial had entered the fabric of culture, it wasn't until years later that it would generate its own subcultural mythos and ideological reality. The contemporary UFO subculture can ultimately find itself in the modern era.

Hugo Gernsback, in 1926, launched the popular magazine, *Amazing Stories*. Over the decades, the magazine consistently featured tales from outer space and other science fiction. In 1938, the magazine was sold to Ziff Davis. Needing to refresh the more dry and academic portions of the magazine, Davis hired Raymond Palmer as editor. In 1943, Palmer received a letter from Richard Shaver claiming that he had discovered an ancient language known as "Mantong." Claiming that it was a proto-language from an ancient race, Shaver claimed that it was the source of all human language. Perhaps seeing an opportunity to spice up his magazine's dwindling readership, or perhaps honestly believing Shaver, Palmer asked Shaver how he discovered this language. What ensued was a series of stories that not only gained readership numbers for *Amazing Stories*, but culturally tied together significant portions of the UFO narrative.

The infamous Shaver Mystery was born and told a complicated tale of an ancient race that lived on Earth but was forced underground by solar radiation. While much of this ancient race left Earth for other planetary homes, some remained behind. Eons of subterranean living divided this advanced ancient race into two distinct groups; the Teros, humanlike and noble, and Deros, evil and sadistic. Shaver, claiming to have spent time as a prisoner of the Deros, wrote this story down in a ten-thousand-word article called *"A Warning to Future Man."*

Palmer, using Shaver's material, expanded the original piece, added significant dramatic action, and retitled it, *"I Remember Lemuria!"* Interestingly, the Lemurians were one of the original races first written about by Blavatsky in her Theosophic texts. The new and updated version of the story was published in the magazine in 1945. This highly successful and legendary issue quickly sold out. The Shaver Mystery stories, which, the magazine suggested, were based on fact, included episodes of alien abduction, various saucer and cigar shaped spacecraft, space aliens, medical experiments, ray guns, cloning, and mind control. The Internet Archive houses digital copies of *Amazing Stories* magazine. [62] I highly recommend visiting the website, and much of the Shaver content was published between 1945 and 1948.

Since the magazine's inception, people have read about the adventures of men fighting aliens deep inside mysterious caverns hidden in the Earth's crust, or aliens from Mars blasting their victims with laser guns. Folklorist Dr. David Clarke points out that these stories "anticipated every motif that would later appear in UFO literature." [63] Furthermore, there are significant links between theosophical texts and the Shaver mysteries.

The general understanding is that contemporary ufology began in the late 1940s. Many UFO researchers point to the famous Kenneth Arnold sighting in 1947 as a pivotal moment in ufological history. Arnold was flying his small aircraft near Mount Rainier in Washington State when he witnessed nine strange objects flying at an incredible rate of speed. He reported his sighting to the press, and newspaper headlines across North America ran articles describing the objects as "flying saucers." According to Greenwood and Dean:

[62] Amazing Stories archive. https://archive.org/details/amazingstoriesmagazine
[63] Clarke, David. "Extraordinary Experiences with UFOs." *The Ashgate Research Companion to Paranormal Cultures.* Routledge. 2014, 79.

The American press had given serious attention to [Arnold's] report over other occasional sightings of aerial objects in the previous several years. Why this was so is the subject of speculation but the timing, for whatever reason, was perfect... The public was ready for a new, exciting interest and flying saucers were it.

Piggybacking off this event was the famous Roswell crash, which occurred a month later in the New Mexico desert. While the event of Roswell is complex and has generated its fair share of mythology and wild speculation, something did slam into the sand that day in July. Whether it was a high-altitude balloon or an alien spacecraft, the world was treated, for a brief moment, to a press release by the United States Air Force confirming the capture of a "flying saucer." A media frenzy followed, but the entire event became forgotten when the military recanted, claimed it was an error, a bit of a joke, and one big misunderstanding.

It is interesting to note that one of the earliest official mentions of a possible otherworldly threat regarding UFOs was not from the United States, but from Sweden. The Swedish Air Intelligence Service drafted a classified assessment of an anomalous aerial phenomenon commonly known as ghost rockets, for its top brass. The memo stated that:

> ...reliable and technically qualified people have reached the conclusion that 'these phenomena are obviously the result of a high technical skill which cannot be credited to any presently known culture on Earth.' They are therefore assuming that these objects originate from some previously unknown or unidentified technology, possible outside the Earth.[64]

These ghost rocket events occurred before the Arnold sighting and Roswell Incident. The problem is that this official document was not released to the public until 1997.

As a result of these events, and a growing number of UFO reports, the American Air Force, and other military bodies around the world, initiated various studies of the UFO phenomenon such as Project Sign, Grudge, and Blue Book. Civilian organizations formed as well, and

---

[64] USAFE Item 14, TT 1524, (Top Secret), 4 November 1948, declassified 1997, National Archives, Washington D.C. See: Dolan, Richard. *UFOs for the 21st Century Mind*. Richard Dolan Press. USA. 2014, 122 .

scientific committees were struck to assess the UFO situation. All this led to one startling but predictable conclusion; no one had any clue what was going on.

While most speculation concerning these objects focused on secret Soviet technology, this hypothesis would not stand the test of time according to Greenwood and Dean:

> With the fading influence of secret weapons as an explanation, something the military couldn't demonstrate to the satisfaction of the U.S. public, thoughts about the origin of flying saucers were thrown wide open. 1948 saw a pilot killed in an alleged saucer encounter and later in the summer an airliner's encounter with a strange object was openly compared to something out of Buck Rogers, a science fiction hero. A solid connection between outer space aliens and flying saucers was building.

The mix of historical events and fictional stories began to shape the UFO myth. A framework was beginning to form. Journalistic magazines also began to play a role in this ideological construction zone. In 1949, True Magazine, out of New York, published an article by Major Donald Keyhoe, who stated that the flying saucers were from outer space. While that article garnered significant attention, on April 7th 1952, Life Magazine published its famous UFO issue. The magazine cover bore the beautiful Marilyn Monroe, and, in the top right corner, the words, "There is a Case for Interplanetary Saucers." Being one of the most influential magazines of its day, the famous article, entitled *"Have We Visitors from Space?"* written by H. B. Darrach Jr. and Robert Ginna, was one of the first mainstream and popular official statements that perhaps, just perhaps, all these UFOs are extraterrestrial in origin. The article establishes that many high quality UFO events are not delusion or hoaxes, and concludes:

> Who, or what, is aboard? Where do they come from? Why are they here? What are the intentions of the beings who control them? Before these awesome questions, science—and mankind—can yet only halt in wonder. Answers may come in a generation—or tomorrow. Somewhere in the dark skies there may be those who know.[65]

---

[65] Darrach H.B. and Ginna Robert. *Have We Visitors from Space?* LIFE Magazine, April 7, 1952 Available online at https://www.nicap.org/life52.htm

The resounding impact of this article cannot be overstated. Not only does it explore, for the first time, an ET connection to the UFO question, but cites several military sources and policies in regard to UFOs. Contentious or not, accurate or not, it heavily seeded the minds of mainstream audiences that these pesky flying saucers may be something from up there. Greenwood and Dean state that this article caused a significant cultural shift:

> Probably not coincidentally, sightings rose to the point of near national panic, culminating in reports of radar tracking of unknown objects over Washington, D.C. The U.S. Air Force felt it necessary to defuse the idea that aliens were here for the simple fact that such speculation would cast doubt on the defensive abilities of the military and that this speculation was circumstantial and not proven... Aliens were firmly in people's thoughts whenever the topic was raised, as declarations from authority were not enough to dissuade such a sensational concept.

The academic community remained pretty quiet on the subject as a general rule, and, when asked by journalists, many simply dismissed the UFO situation as nothing more than hoaxes or mistaken identity. However, a few rogue academics did choose to engage with the phenomenon. The 1950s through to the 1970s saw some astronomers, physicists, and scientists such as J. Allen Hynek, Carl Sagan, James McDonald, Jacques Vallée and Donald Menzel at least broach the subject in academic discourse. Obviously, not all of them came to the same conclusions. Physicist James McDonald addressed the possibility that UFOs were extraterrestrial in origin, while Hynek saw the scientific benefit of studying UFOs but was rather reserved in his judgements concerning alien contact. Carl Sagan believed that it was highly unlikely that UFOs were alien spacecraft, while Vallée posited that psychosocial control system was at work. Menzel basically said the whole extraterrestrial thing was unfounded hokum.[66]

While a handful of scientists explored the UFO issue, the widespread belief was that UFOs and their pilots, whoever they were, were not objectively real. *The Condon Report* of 1968, based out of the University of Colorado, pushed this line of thinking. While the report was,

---

[66] Eghigian, Greg. *Making UFOs make sense: Ufology, Science and the History of their Mutual Mistrust.* Public Understanding of Science Journal. 1-15. 2015 .

and still is, heavily criticized by members of the UFO community, Edward Condon, the lead researcher concluded that "nothing has come from the study of UFOs in the past 21 years that has added to scientific knowledge."[67] Regardless of the report's contents, which included many well investigated aerial phenomena that the scientists concluded were truly unknown, any official examination of the UFO phenomenon died with Condon's words, and UFO research was forced to slink off into the night. Never again would it be granted access to the halls of mainstream academia and the sciences.

However, neither Condon's report, nor any official or academic downplaying of the UFO phenomenon, curbed its continued and elusive presence. The second half of the 1960s saw a significant rise in witnesses coming forward to report sightings, and even describe extraterrestrial contact and abduction. Antonio Villas Boas who was allegedly abducted in the late 1950s, and then into the 1960s with Betty and Barney Hill, the Andreasson abduction, and others. These became and remain landmark cases, and, while skeptics doubt their legitimacy, they still come up in conversation within UFO circles.

Indeed, after the "flying saucer" crash at Roswell, the public mind began to speculate as to the source of this amazing technology. Many came to a predictable conclusion: "if it isn't from here, then where?" The funny thing about history, especially in regard to culture, is that fiction can be just as influential as fact.

Journalists and fiction authors, as well as others, would help to drive a belief in extraterrestrials, and link that belief to objective and real UFO events. The rise of visual media, such as popular cinema and television in the fifties and sixties, would also have had significant impact on the cultural and individual's perception of UFO events. Films such as *The Day the Earth Stood Still (1951)*, *War of the Worlds (1953)*, and *Invasion of the Body Snatchers (1956)* would have generated additional UFO imagery. Robbie Graham, author of *Silver Screen Saucers*, points out that:

> Ufological entertainment products have assumed permanent residency in the popular consciousness, and thus will always occupy at least some level of our perceived reality... Whether or not they serve to

---

[67] Condon. EU and Gillmor DS. *Scientific Study of Unidentified Flying Objects*. Bantam Press. New York. 1969. Available at http://files.ncas.org/condon/index.html

fictionalize or actualize, what is clear is that movies of any genre inform our 'understanding' of the world around us."[68]

Graham's statement, here, brings to the forefront the connections, which history, mythology, storytelling, and ideology have upon what is considered "real." To suggest that the UFO subculture is based upon some kernel of objective truth or reality is not only impossible, but also foolish. Rather, UFO subculture is a collective reality where truth and fiction coexist simultaneously. It is our first example of Derrida's ghost, the foundation of events, both historical and mythological, factual and fictional, pushing the boundary of what is known and understood but, furthermore, for the UFO community, muddying the water of ideology.

The development of cultural ideologies, particularly for subcultures, is incredibly nuanced and complex. There is no watershed event, which led to the current paradigm concerning the links between UFOs and beings from outer space. While one can write out a laundry list of important historical events and UFO sightings, no single event is responsible for what is known today in UFO circles as the *extraterrestrial hypothesis,* nor how the entire subculture was shaped. Rather, one must look at how the history and popular cultural milieu led to this ideological shift. We must also understand that subcultures themselves evolve with history, and that those subcultures shape history itself, and often in strange ways. While objective historical events occur, it is not always clear how those events affect the cultural and social psyche of people living during them. We can try to understand the event, but not always its impact. There is no way to separate UFO events from the collective interpretation of those events. More importantly, the UFO event is *made real* by that collective interpretation. The two, object and subject, are in symbiosis.

The UFO phenomenon is shaped by the melding of real and objective UFO encounters, and fictional cultural myths. What occurs is a symbiosis of ideologies. Fact merges with fiction. The real event intermingles with the representations of the event in culture. Greenwood and Dean conclude by asking a simple question, "Flying saucers influencing man's culture or man's culture influencing flying saucers?"

The history of UFO discourse, and the resulting subculture, is founded upon this duality. The history of the UFO is both objective and subjective—a real phenomenon filtered through a cultural and social lens, which, in turn, shapes the phenomenon. As theorist William Dewan

---

[68] Graham, Robbie. *Silver Screen Saucers.* White Crow Books. 2015, 13.

points out, "the UFO tradition is founded on real, often strange, experiences that both inform and are formed by existing cultural traditions and mental schemas."[69]

The UFO subculture exists within an ever shifting and changing framework of myths, ideologies, and history. The vast majority of UFO discourse exists within this landscape, a constant interplay of simultaneous fiction and fact. The history of UFO discourse and the formation of the contemporary subculture bring us to this mythological realm, this place where ideologies reign. Herein lies the creative and spellbinding beauty of the UFO community and, to many within that community, its inherent ugly flaw.

UFO researcher Lorin Cutts calls this the *UFO mythological zone*. The mythological zone is "the gap between fact and belief, what we see and what we want to see, and what we experience and how we interpret it."[70] Cutts believes that this divide between truth and fiction is responsible for dysfunction inside the UFO subculture.[71] He explains:

> ... look at ufology as a whole, the vast majority lies within this mythological zone. And while there is nothing wrong with open discussion, speculation, and hypothesizing in a field so vast and mysterious, there is a world of difference between these things and passing off totally unfounded statements as absolutes.[72]

Cutts touches upon exactly what cultural theorists study when it comes to the mythologies that exist around and within a subculture. This mythological ideology forms the reality of the subculture.

This does not mean that UFOs are made up stories with no objective place in the physical world. Carl Jung points out that many myths are based upon, or seem to occur alongside, "meteorological and other natural phenomena." However, he points out that these objective and natural events often offer little to explain why or how that myth forms or functions. Jung concluded: "Should it be that an unknown

---

[69] William J. Dewan. ""A Saucerful of Secrets": An Interdisciplinary Analysis of UFO Experiences." *The Journal of American Folklore* 119, no. 472 (2006): 184-202. http://www.jstor.org/stable/4137923.

[70] Graham, Robbie (ed), *UFOs: Reframing the Debate*, White Crow Books, 2017, 81.

[71] Ibid, 82.

[72] Ibid, 81.

physical phenomenon is the outward cause of the myth, this would detract nothing from the myth...[73]

The cultural perception of real UFO events shapes those events. It becomes impossible to differentiate between the paradigms, which exist within UFO discourse, and UFOs themselves. This is not to say that people who have had encounters with UFOs or alleged extraterrestrials did not experience those events objectively, rather, the interpretation of those events is filtered by their cultural background and ideological lens. They are, as Jung points out, experiencing a "living myth."[74] What author and UFO researcher Jacques Vallée calls "folklore in the making."[75]

The UFO, as a *real* object, and the subculture are both forced into the gap between fact and illusion. If the subculture is the machine, which generates ufological ideology, then the UFO is the ghost within that machine. However, the symbiosis between object and subject, the UFO and the subculture, the UFO as a phenomenon is also influenced by the subculture. Does this then mean that the UFO is the machine haunted by the UFO community? Here we see *différance* in action. The more the UFO subculture attempts to define and clarify the UFO enigma, the more we defer and differ the objective UFO. The Derridean ghost manifests before us: *both are machines to be haunted, and both do the haunting.*

---

[73] Jung, Carl. *Flying Saucers.* Routledge: UK. 1959, 19.

[74] Ibid, 11.

[75] Vallée, Jacques. *Passport to Magonia.* Daily Grail Press. Australia. 1969, 159.

CHAPTER 13

Controlling the Narrative

I want to address a few key ideas, which play a role in framing the UFO subculture. First, the belief on the part of mainstream culture that the UFO subculture is fundamentally tied to the extraterrestrial visitor hypothesis. In truth, the countless and varying UFO reports tend to point to something potentially much more complicated. Secondly, how this belief has pushed the UFO subculture onto the cultural edge and forced it to be a taboo subject. Finally, the irony of how the UFO community is alienated, yet programs such as the Search for Extraterrestrial Intelligence are not.

The mainstream interpretation of the "extraterrestrial" is predominantly a physical being from another planet, however, in reality, the UFO subculture has many variations of what exactly an "extraterrestrial" is. David Clarke asserts that, "...the UFO myth is complex and consists of a number of interlinked legends, individual narratives, and metanarratives."[76]

Perhaps the most prolific and compelling viewpoint, at least to me, is that of Jacques Vallée, best summed up by Jeffrey Kripal, author of *Authors of the Impossible:*

> What Jacques Vallée came to know, in other words, could not be explained as something strictly objective or subjective. It was both.

---

[76] Clarke, David. "Extraordinary Experiences with UFOs". *The Ashgate Research Companion to Paranormal Cultures*. Routledge. 2014, 89.

And it was neither. When Vallée writes of the paranormal... he is not thinking of purely internal states or subjective conditions, however interesting and profound... He is thinking of something that is mythical and physical, spiritual and material at the same time.[77]

The UFO phenomenon itself often defies the physical and material, yet clearly maintains a physical presence. Perhaps it is both material and immaterial, or perhaps it is neither, but something else entirely? Here, again, we see the concept of the ghost come to haunt us; this phenomenon is not necessarily this or that, but neither and both simultaneously. Before we explore deeper into this, we must address how cultural interpretation has affected the subculture. No matter how strange or esoteric the UFO narrative can be, the subculture is imprisoned by a materialist ideology.

The aliens and the stories concerning a witness encounter, often depicted in film, television, or in literature, over-simplifies the narrative. This mainstream interpretation permeates the mainstream cultural fabric and generates the ideological illusion that the UFO subculture believes that flesh and blood aliens are visiting Earth in their technologically superior space ships.

German philosopher Theodor Adorno argues that modern day belief in the supernatural and, by extension, extraterrestrials, is a "secondary superstition." Simply put, the general public largely gathers its knowledge on the paranormal "through the mediation" of mainstream media. The countless UFO documentaries and television programs that dot Netflix and the History Channel are such examples. These information sources are typically accepted as "reliable sources of advice," but, as Adorno points out, are driven by significant bias. He writes that popular media has viewers "accept" paranormal phenomena "because it exists, without much reflection." However, these programs cater to certain ideologies and paradigms because the viewer must, in a sense, buy in. He writes that an audience will only accept the idea "provided... that their own psychological demands somehow correspond to the offer."

In other words, the mainstream public, those not in the subculture, interpret the UFO phenomenon in a "secondary" way; not directly, such as seeing a UFO or having a close encounter, but via documentaries, television shows, YouTube channels, and other cultural texts that

---

[77] Kripal, Jeffrey. "Authors of the Impossible: The Paranormal and the Sacred." University of Chicago: Chicago. 2010, 146.

portray those events. These programs typically carry with them a specific interpretation and oversimplify the nuance of the phenomenon.

Adorno continues:

> ... the individual's own primary experience with the occult [or the UFO phenomenon], whatever its psychological meaning and roots or its validity, rarely, if ever, enter the social phenomenon to which our studies are devoted. Here the occult [or UFO encounter] appears rather institutionalized, objectified and, to a large extent, socialized... people responding to the stimuli... seem in a way "alien" to the experience on which they claim their decisions are based.

Adorno points out that the effect of mediating the paranormal via popular media sanitizes the phenomenon. It becomes part of the social and cultural system of ideologies and simplified in order to be consumed by popular audiences.

The UFO phenomenon, as presented via popular media, is inauthentic. It is an altered message, removed from its genuine state, washed and stripped of its originality, and sanitized for palatability. The result is that mainstream culture interprets the UFO phenomenon, and the subculture, which studies and engages that phenomenon, as being "alien." It becomes a sideshow of freaks, rather than a portrayal of human beings who have experienced something anomalous and strange.

The larger issue is that this oversimplified message only pushes UFO discourse further into the fringes of culture, reinforcing an already established taboo. Rather than portraying the UFO subculture as a community of people with varying experiences, hypotheses, and rationales that continuously debate with one another, the media presents a single interpretation: an interpretation that forces the mainstream public to assume that all who are interested in the topic believe in alien beings from other planets. It is easier to taboo and alienate a community when it appears to be unified. The voices of actual members of the UFO community, and the people who have had alleged experiences with the phenomenon itself, are unable to have their voices heard when it counters the ideological framework portrayed in popular media, or re-enforced by academic, scientific or political institutions. Much like any group of people with disenfranchised ideologies, the mainstream "alienates" the members of the UFO subculture. It paints them as outsiders.

The actual ideologies within the UFO subculture are diverse. Many within the UFO field have a wide variety of interpretations concerning the alleged intelligent entities behind the UFO phenomenon. Furthermore, many within the UFO community do not make claims concerning alien visitation at all, and suggest something interdimensional, spiritual or mystical as the cause. Others would argue that all UFO sightings are prosaic, advanced human technology, or something natural yet to be fully understood by science. While a small segment of the UFO community may be paranoid tinfoil hat wearing zealots, many take a level-headed approach to a very anomalous phenomenon that refuses to go away.

It seems strangely natural to assume that the UFO community is made up of a bunch of lunatics because they believe in aliens, and any alternative to this line of reasoning seems awkward. It *feels* funny to concede that possibly, just possibly, the people who concern themselves with the *alien Other* might be on to something. It is as if the mere idea of visitation counters some spooky inherent logic and innate rationality. There are no such things as aliens, right?

This feeling, this discomfort, is fueled by a tendency for individuals to lean towards a groupthink consensus reality. Popular media reinforces the alien myth, and, with the help of academics and scientists, ensures that the concept of the alien remains uncomfortable enough to be laughed at, but comfortable enough not to cause too much anxiety. The role of the broader culture, whether it is the mainstream media, academia, or any group in a position of cultural power, is to attempt to remove the UFO phenomenon and the subculture from its dualistic gap: in other words, to keep the issue physical and material. They wish to exorcize the ghost, as it were.

We arrive at a hypocritical cultural juxtaposition: if UFOs or extraterrestrials are not to be taken seriously by anyone outside of the UFO subculture, why do other scientific programs that deal with exoplanets or searching for extraterrestrial life continue to receive support from popular media and scientific academia?

CHAPTER 14

Scientism and the *Myth of Truth*

~

M any within scientific communities generally accept that life
exists elsewhere in the cosmos. In 1960, Dr. Frank Drake cob-
bled together the famous Drake Equation, which attempted
to calculate the rate at which life would form, potentially reach intelligence, and become technologically able to communicate.

The Drake Equation is: $N = R * fp * ne * fl * fi * fc * L$.

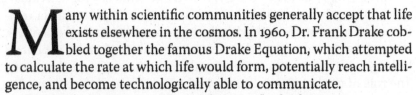

N is the number of detectable civilizations in the Milky Way galaxy.
R is the rate of star formation in the galaxy.
fp is the fraction of stars that form planets.
ne is the number of planets hospitable to life (i.e., Earth-like planets).
fl is the fraction of these planets on which life actually emerges.
fi is the fraction of these planets on which intelligent life arises.
fc is the fraction of these planets with intelligent beings capable of
interstellar communication.
L is the length of time such a civilization remains detectable.[78]

The scientific community, comprising predominantly those who work
with the Search for Extraterrestrial Intelligence, or SETI, accepts this
equation as one of the essential tools in understanding the rate at
which intelligent life may develop. As humanity learns more about

---

[78] The Drake Equation. http://www.seti.org/drakeequation

astronomy and physics, the above variables change, however, as the SETI website states:

> ... the Drake Equation is a simple, effective tool for stimulating intellectual curiosity about the universe around us, for helping us to understand that life as we know it is the end product of a natural, cosmic evolution, and for making us realize how much we are a part of that universe. A key goal of the SETI Institute is to further high quality research that will yield additional information related to any of the factors of this fascinating equation... any practical search for distant intelligent life must necessarily be a search for some manifestation of a distant technology. In each of its last four decadal reviews, the National Research Council has emphasized the relevance and importance of searching for evidence of the electromagnetic signature of distant civilizations."[79]

There is a clear justification for this equation, and, furthermore, a respected scientific organization using it as justification for research and funding. This should give one pause. Doesn't this equation, and the entire SETI project, hinge upon a massive presupposition? The Drake Equation is not proof of alien life; it is simply a hypothetical equation, a really well written "best guess." How is SETI able to justify its time and treasure upon such a flimsy foundation?

One could argue that SETI, and science in general, looks at objective evidence. It uses objective tools to measure the world in an objective way. Radio telescopes, spectrometers, and radar are all examples of tools that provide basic measurable data, which can be checked and rechecked. One may suggest that SETI's project is legitimate because the data collected is objective, and not hinging upon belief in spacemen. However, all of that data needs to be interpreted by scientists, and those scientists come to the table with systems of belief and cultural baggage, just like everyone else, and assert that the data must fit within pre-established models. While the data may be objective, the perception of that data certainly is not.

SETI's entire project is based upon the simple hypothesis that extraterrestrials exist, and they are, or were, emitting signals into space, which can be intercepted by human telescopes. Furthermore, additional assumptions are made to suggest that these extraterrestrials use certain types of radio signals. Focusing the search to certain star

---

[79] Ibid.

systems, monitoring certain frequencies and not others is even more speculation. The entire project is speculative, based on a hypothesis, and there is no certainty in any of it.

The project continues and is seen as a noble effort towards a broader understanding of the universe. However, when we truly break down the SETI project, do we not see the giant elephant (or alien for that matter) in the room? It is nothing but guesswork. Following this, is it so preposterous to suggest that those extraterrestrials are possibly visiting Earth? Wouldn't the continued and consistent influx of reports concerning odd aerial lights, eerie visitations by strange beings, or other anomalous activity be essentially more evidence than SETI itself has ever provided, or needed, to justify its own existence?

Suggesting that the SETI project is legitimate, while the study of UFOs is illegitimate, is a form of cultural cognitive dissonance. If the idea of aliens is absurd, why do scientific projects that aim to find otherworldly intelligence receive funding? This is not to say that the scientific community should scrap the SETI project. Indeed, humanity should make every attempt to further its understanding of the cosmos. Rather, what we bump into is not so much the scientific search for extraterrestrials, but the general anxiety we feel towards some incomprehensible *Other* and the community that works towards seeking that *Other.*

Before proceeding further, one must shake off the preconception that the UFO phenomenon must be material in origin; that is, the limiting view that flesh and blood aliens from, say, Zeta Reticuli are travelling in space ships to reach Earth. This is simply one notion, and one that has been swallowed up by the mainstream. There is much more to consider and many more hypotheses. Instead, approach with an open mind; with an *I don't know* mentality.

It is not that science takes issue with the idea of extraterrestrials, as SETI is clearly engaged in this type of work, but that science takes issue with people who believe in their visitation of Earth. Previously, we underscored the symbiotic historical and ideological framework in which the UFO subculture exists. These mechanisms have ensured the ostracizing of the subculture from mainstream and popular culture. Extraterrestrials, as a mythos and construct, play a role in this, but it is not only the idea of extraterrestrials that has pushed the UFO community to the edges of culture, but that mainstream culture demands the UFO community exists on that edge. To official and mainstream culture, the anomaly is not the problem, but the people who point it out. In other words, it's not the aliens so much, but the UFO community itself.

These narrative foundations of the UFO phenomenon have made "extraterrestrial" a dirty word and, through transitive property, the term "UFO" as well. Later in this book, I will engage with the countercultural aspects of the UFO subculture, but, for now, we must understand that the community itself is pushed out of popular discourse and debate by these ideologies. Even though there are varying interpretations within the subculture of what UFOs are, the mythology, which surrounds the subculture, limits those differing ideologies and hypotheses to escape into mainstream understanding. Total knowledge about a subculture is impossible; however, understanding that subculture's place within social context helps in deconstructing its illusions. The extraterrestrial, as a concept, is an outsider to humanity. The UFO subculture, by association, is an outsider to broader mainstream culture.

Extraterrestrials, whether they are physical beings or more mystical in nature, pose no real threat to scientific knowledge. To the established academia, those beings are far, far away. Furthermore, their arrival here, should they exist, would only broaden scientific understanding for all of humanity. If aliens landed tomorrow, announced their presence, and took credit for centuries of visitation, would the often criticized pseudoscientific and reductionist field of ufology and UFO discourse die an instant death? Would the study of alien technology, their transportation, and the aliens themselves, become an established academic and scientific discourse? Supposing such an event occurred, no matter how unlikely, the study of which would undoubtedly become established into schools of philosophy, sociology, theology, and the other humanities. The UFO subculture only exists because the entirety of the phenomenon remains *unknown*. It is due to this unknowability that the community is not allowed to participate in established academic and official culture. Furthermore, it is the mythology that has formed around this unknowability that has shaped the subculture into such a vast collection of ideologies and people.

It is not that the UFO community is made up of kooks. Every group has its fair share of kookiness, but that the people who make up the subculture challenge the authority of the very sciences and academics they want to impress. They are 'kooks' because they do not agree with the often dogmatic and arbitrary control the sciences have upon mainstream culture. When scientists, like Dr. Neil deGrasse Tyson, the late Carl Sagan, and Mr. Bill Nye, state that extraterrestrials are not visiting Earth, we learn much about their cultural ideology and the limitations of their role as pop culture scientists. Perhaps more interestingly, by openly attacking the UFO question, they inadvertently ensure the survival of the discourse. By engaging in the UFO debate, as Jodi Dean points out, they establish that there is something worth engaging.[80] That being said, we do not gain much insight into the existence of extraterrestrials, or any legitimate progress in thinking, merely their cultural bias.

This cultural bias was apparent after Harvard University professor and psychiatrist John Mack published his famous book, *Abduction: Human Encounters with Aliens* in 1994. Mack was heavily criticized by his peers for promoting nonsense, and, as historian Greg Eghigian, points out, his colleagues suggested, using quite an inappropriate racial trope, that he was "going native" by working with abductees and members of the UFO community.[81] According to Eghigian, the controversy surrounding Mack's work began when he started to "believe" his patients, and accept that perhaps some intelligence was behind the tales they recounted. According to Mack:

> What the abduction phenomenon has led me (I would say now inevitably) to see is that we participate in a universe or universes that are filled with intelligences from which we have cut ourselves off, having lost the senses by which we might know them. It has become clear to me also that our restricted worldview or paradigm lies behind most of the major destructive patterns that threaten the human future—mindless corporate acquisitiveness that perpetuates vast differences between rich and poor and contributes to hunger and disease; ethnonational violence resulting in mass killing which could grow into nuclear holocaust; and ecological destruction on a scale that threatens the survival of the earth's living systems.[82]

Whether Mack's patients were truly being taken by extraterrestrials is not important here. What is important is that Mack directly challenged academic and scientific authority. Rather than conducting

[80] Dean, Jodi, 55.

[81] Eghigian, Greg. *The Psychiatrist, the Aliens, and "Going Native".* Psychiatric Times. 2014. Accessed January 2018. http://www.psychiatrictimes.com/blogs/history-psychiatry/psychiatrist-aliens-and-going-native

[82] Mack, John. *Abduction: Human Encounters with Aliens.* Simon and Schuster. 1994. Quote taken from article *The Psychiatrist, the Aliens, and "Going Native"* by G. Eghigian.

proper and thorough inquiry into his findings, his community lumped him into the lunatic fringe UFO subculture and attributed his new-found world view to a colonial cultural trope. Furthermore, it only reinforces the ideological fears, which haunt the academic and scientific communities, that contemporary Western materialist thinking is somehow flawed.

This bias problem is ancient. Plato, the Greek philosopher, explores these limitations in the allegory of the cave. A person who is born and raised in a cave their entire lives and is only shown shadows of the world projected onto the wall by a fire, believes that scene to be reality. If, released from this prison, they venture outside and see the world for what it truly is, would the others in the cave believe their story if they returned to tell them? Would the others in the cave shift their perception of reality, or would they choose to stay in the darkness?

In dealing with the construct of the extraterrestrial, we come to a very specific conclusion: it, whatever *it* may be, directly challenges our reality. Much like the ghost, it problematizes a duality that we inherently assume to be natural. The UFO and the alien are both present and absent, real and illusion, but to us, the two call into question the illusionary difference between human and non-human. I must briefly touch on the construct of the extraterrestrial.

It must be recognized that the UFO and the extraterrestrial are essentially "uncannily familiar and concrete"[83] to our culture. As anthropologist Debbora Battaglia suggests, the alien *other* is a "lived experience."[84] It is a construct that is everywhere. The alien, and the flying saucer, appears in film and television, video games, corporate logos, beverage containers, laptop stickers, smartphone cases, and much more. It is entrenched in the reality of popular culture, and, perhaps more interestingly, under the control of human economic and social systems. One can possess the alien or the UFO, buy it, wear it or slap it on a backpack. I can master the *Other* and take ownership over it.

Battaglia points out that this "ET effect" is intersubjective,[85] and even though a whole subculture exists which potentially challenges the mainstream, the flesh and blood alien itself comes from a very human origin. UFO cults, conspiracy theorists and ufologists are

---

[83] Battaglia, Debbora. "Insiders' Voices in Outerspaces." in *E.T. Culture: Anthropology in Outerspaces.* Duke University Press. 2005, 1.

[84] Ibid.

[85] Ibid, 2.

"prospecting starward for social connection... being both of this world and out of it."[86]

As a social concept, it is a total outsider. The philosopher Michael Zimmerman refers to the alien as the "radically different other,"[87] but, even more fundamentally problematic, a *superior other*. The narrative paints the extraterrestrial as powerful, possessing more intelligence, and therefore, more agency over rule, power and control than humans. They remove humanity, and all that goes with it, from the peak of cosmic evolution. Humans, their achievements and social systems, would drop one link in the food chain.

Zimmerman refers to this idea as *anthropocentric humanism*. The fundamental belief system that humans have "superiority over other life."[88] By using European conquest and colonialism as an example, Zimmerman proposes an interesting idea. He writes: "Having treated allegedly inferior human others so ferociously a few centuries ago, how might Westerners expect to be treated if discovered and colonized by technologically superior others?"[89]

While an "end of days" scenario may be extreme, the extraterrestrial construct does pose significant danger to established social and ideological order, primarily the control that science has over knowledge itself. Battagila writes:

> In a positive vein, the idea of an alien knowledge source can inspire bold efforts of translation across differences, carrying the promise of more closely articulated social exchange... In a negative vein, alien powers can call up a common nemesis: the opaque and inaccessible "powers that be"... who guard access to knowledge.[90]

Unfortunately for the subculture, those *powers that be*, the people who maintain the illusion of official culture, do not view the alien question, or the whole ufological discourse, in a positive light. While Battaglia may argue that there exists a positive ideology concerning

---

[86] Ibid, 3.

[87] Zimmerman. Michael. "Encountering Alien Otherness." *The Concept of the Foreign*, ed Rebecca Saunders. Lexington Books. Maryland. 2002, 153.

[88] Ibid, 157.

[89] Ibid, 158.

[90] Battaglia, 7.

the extraterrestrial, that optimism is typically existent only within the UFO subculture itself, and not generally outside of it.

While the discovery or some public annunciation of alien existence would shift scientific thinking, and perhaps even provide significant leaps in scientific knowledge, we must understand that the extraterrestrial would potentially undo the cultural control, which science has. Science, as a field of human endeavor, would only benefit from the proven existence of a visiting Other. Science, as a social system, which arbitrates ideology, would be altered permanently if not destroyed. The establishment of Science would lose its stranglehold on what is considered "knowledge."

The construct of Science initially established itself as a revolution against the ontological control established by the Catholic Church. Science wrestled the cultural and social control of knowledge from God and the Vatican to educated—and therefore elite—lay people. The power and control, which knowledge provide, after the scientific revolutions of The Renaissance and Enlightenment, no longer came from the divine, but from humanity itself. Humans became the absolute arbiters of knowledge, and that arbitration consolidates the dogmatism, and, more importantly, the power of science. According to scientific cosmology, the universe is no longer resting upon the divine, but upon the material. Zimmerman writes that:

> Modern science has not only discouraged the belief in God and cosmic purpose, but has also encouraged people to conceive of human life primarily in terms of survival, for which the acquisition of power over others is essential.[91]

Science has essentially generated an anthropocentric view of the universe, in that the agency, logic, and reasoning of humanity are the peak of cosmic evolution. Furthermore, the subsequent effects of that evolution are humanity's social hierarchy and institutions: science being of the highest importance. Zimmerman cites physicist Paul Davies' opinion that the discovery of extraterrestrial life would provide humanity with a rebirth. Science, in its cold calculations, often paints humanity and our "pale blue dot" as an infinitely inconsequential speck of dust in the universe. Should humanity ever realize that intelligent life exists elsewhere in the stars, this would "give us cause to believe that

---

[91] Ibid, 163

we, in our humble way, are part of a larger, majestic process of cosmic self-knowledge."[92]

To suggest that there exists something greater, some *superior Other*, casts doubt upon science's control over knowledge. If science has become a religion, the notion of extraterrestrials visiting Earth is heresy. More importantly, science's greatest achievement, the modern effigy of technology, which we all bow before, would potentially pale in comparison to that of the *Other*, or worse, be deemed a curious mythical or mystical process which rests totally, or at least partially, outside of sole human ingenuity. The worthiness of science, its universal and supposed objective power, is cast into doubt. Science, as the ideology machine, would be forced to defer its authority to alien outsiders, but, even more problematic, other disciplines that do not share a scientific worldview. Those who oppose myth and belief as remnants of a supposed bygone era would see their own mythology collapse at their feet; scientific reality and legitimacy would be called into question and their manifest destiny would come to an end.

Perhaps less dramatic is the essential state of language itself within the supposed objectivity of science. George P. Hansen, author of *The Trickster and The Paranormal* cites philosopher Roland Barthes:

> As far as science is concerned language is simply an instrument, which it profits it to make as transparent and neutral as possible: it is subordinate to the matter of science (workings, hypotheses, results) which, so it is said, exists outside language and precedes it.

Barthes points out that the religiosity of science has purposefully gone out of its way to regress language, to subjugate it. From the 16th century onwards:

> The corporate blossoming of empiricism, rationalism and an evidential religion (with the Reformation), that is, of the scientific spirit in the widest sense of the term, should have been accompanied by a regression in the autonomy of language.[93]

What must be made very clear is that language itself forms our

---

[92] Davis. Paul. *Are We Alone?* Basic books. New York. 1995, 129.

[93] Barthes, Roland. *Science Versus Literature.* 1967. *From* Hansen, George. *The Trickster and The Paranormal.* Kindle Locations 7039-7046. Xlibris US. Kindle Edition.

ideologies, values, paradigms, cultures and social organization. We, as creatures, are governed by our languages, which create for us an understanding of, and therefore a filter for, our daily reality. If language plays second fiddle to the dogma of science, so too do our thoughts and ideas. We become enslaved to it.

Hansen points out that one of Derrida's most famous literary philosophical tools, *deconstruction*, calls science's hold on language into question. Hansen points out that "meaning is banished from the consciousness of science" but deconstruction points out that meaning is "neither neutral nor transparent." Indeed, as Hansen points out, language precedes science and truly has "primacy over it."[94] Even more, Derridean deconstruction is the very act of unpacking the *différance* which exists within communication and knowledge. It "undoes" the very connection between subject and signifier, in other words, object and the meaning of that object. It asserts that science's claim to objective truth is nothing more than arbitrary ideology agreed upon by consensus rather than some direct link to *capital T a priori "Truth."* It pushes meaning itself into a gap between reality and illusion, that which we cannot know and what we believe to know. It is through Derrida that we can free language from enslavement, and, more importantly, begin to gain ideological freedom on our own terms. To put it simply, an awareness of Derridean *différance* frees us with words that go beyond the numbers of science. We must accept that science itself is as ideological as the people who are convinced of alien visitation. Science is a construct made up of people, all of whom were born into their respective social paradigms. They carry with them their cultural baggage and exist within ideological frameworks. To put it bluntly, scientists, just like the rest of us, are mere mortals. The difference is that they have been granted control over what we constitute as knowledge and essentially dictate what is worth knowing.

I appreciate the boldness of my claim, and, indeed, any knee-jerk skeptics and scientists will most likely guffaw at my suggestion that science is not objective, but ideological. Before moving on, I wish to draw attention to one particular nuts and bolts case where a scientist and his breakthrough serve as an example to my claim above.

Fritz Haber, a Nobel Prize winning chemist, invented the Haber-Bosch process, which allows for the artificial and industrial creation of ammonia using atmospheric nitrogen and hydrogen gas. His work

94 Ibid.

revolutionized the way we fertilize crops, and roughly half of the world's population today relies on food grown using his method of nitrogen fertilizer production. His invention, in no uncertain terms, allowed the fast-growing human population in the early 20th century to survive. In 1918, he was awarded the Nobel Prize in Chemistry for his achievement. Curiously, the same man has also been nicknamed the "father of chemical warfare."

In 1914, Haber led the German chemical science division for the military, which was responsible for the creation of chlorine gas to be used in trench warfare. At the Second Battle of Ypres, which took place in April/May of 1915, Haber was there personally to watch his invention be used against enemy soldiers. Chemical weapons became a major focus of development for the German military during the First World War and was responsible for the death of countless people, both combatants and civilians alike. Haber, a patriotic German, served his country with pride. He was even promoted to the rank of Captain by the Kaiser. In May of 1915, he and his wife, Clara, got into an argument. While one can only speculate what it was about, she herself held a Ph.D. in Chemistry, and was a recently converted Christian. Some historians believe their argument stemmed from his work with chemical weapons. Regardless, using his service pistol, Clara shot herself in the chest in her garden. Curiously, days after her death, Haber left for the Eastern Front to oversee his chlorine gas being used on the Russian army.

Haber never regretted his work in chemical warfare, and even argued once that death was death, no matter how it was inflicted. In one poignant moment, Haber famously reflected that: "During peace time a scientist belongs to the World, but during war time he belongs to his country."

To suggest that science, and scientists themselves, move beyond their social worlds into some "objective" realm is inaccurate. Haber, and many other scientists like him, are driven by the same fears, values and ideas that drive the rest of humanity. Although Haber's science fed millions, when he felt called to serve his country, he felt no regret in using that very same invention to kill. Science as an objective "thing" is merely a social construct made upon the backs of people. There is no "science" without the individuals, the scientists, who "do it." Those individuals rely upon language and culture in order to exist within their social contexts. They are silly humans just like you and me. Much like Haber, they have their ideologies and paradigms, their ghosts, forces that drive them towards their beliefs and values.

Scientists who are critical of those who explore the UFO topic are not critical because of some supposed higher truth, which only they can access. They are not gods who sit up on high with the universe revolving around them. The scientists and UFO debunkers who snicker at the UFO subculture do not do so because of some universal *a priori* truth or rule. Alas, their need to hurl insults and ridicule stems from drives which are much baser. They are critical because even allowing the slightest openness to the topic will put them at risk. Initially, they will, themselves, be lumped into the lunatic fringe. More jarringly, however, they may even begin to shift their perception of reality. The academic and capitalist forces, which govern them, do not allow them to contemplate such realities. It is not the search for truth, which keeps scientists away from the UFO topic, but fear.

I am not suggesting that we throw the baby out with the bathwater. Science is, for all intents and purposes, progress in a positive direction. Science is essential to our continued social survival. It cures illness. It puts people on the Moon. Criticism of the scientific establishment is not tantamount to open rebellion. That being said, we, as a society, have allowed science to form a consensus reality where it is in command of "truth." Instead of pushing away the UFO phenomenon and the attached extraterrestrial Other, it should pursue its study.

Broadly speaking, the inherent issue is that science refuses to get into bed with the people in the UFO community. As I have argued previously, science does not necessarily take issue with the idea of extraterrestrials, rather, it takes issue with the people who are critical of the ideology that science creates, and who challenge the power, which currently it wields. To put it another way, the illusion of objectivity and consensus reality must be maintained.

CHAPTER 15

The Counter-Cultural UFO Community

~

Other facets of established social power systems would also fall victim to a potential ET visitation. As UFO researcher and writer Miguel Romero argues: "The UFO disruption is not only a threat to the authority of scientific orthodoxy, it fundamentally defies every conceivable paradigm that human society is built upon..."[95]

Briefly, we must explore how aliens affect our other cultural institutions. Perhaps the most politically damaging would be towards the concepts of nationhood and government.

Romero points to cases of UFOs hovering over nuclear missile silos, such as the Malmstrom Air Force Base Incident, or zipping through restricted air space. The UFO narrative at times has significant variation, but a few consistent through lines exist. One of those through lines regards the UFO as sovereign object, which seems to have significant diplomatic freedom. The UFO as object does not obey laws regarding sovereign airspace or national borders, nor do the extraterrestrial beings apply for visas before landing on foreign soil to scoop up plant samples, mutilate cows, or abduct people.

---

[95] Graham, Robbie (ed), *UFOs: Reframing the Debate*, White Crow Books, 2017, 153.

If we look at the UFO phenomenon as a whole, the superior Other, whatever it may be and assuming it exists, may not recognize the construct of a national government. Regardless of whether the UFO phenomenon is physical or mystical, the events that seem to present themselves throughout the UFO and contactee narrative indicate extreme technological and/or intellectual abilities. On a broader philosophical level, it is silly to assume that human deference to a ruling body, such as a nation, state, or government, would be the same for another intelligence with a totally separate evolutionary path, assuming that intelligence is even biological to begin with. The concept of "government" is a human construct that appeared via a very specific human political evolution. This does not mean that a political system of governance is universal. In simple terms, we cannot assume that another intelligence would consider government as a legitimate form of social organization, assuming they even have social organization. While government is a fundamental aspect of modern human civilization, it may not exist anywhere but here on Earth.

The result of alien visitation, then, would call into question the concept of nationalism, state loyalty, and even citizenship itself. It would call into question the very nature of society and culture. To put it plainly, humanity could become a planet of stateless refugees. Ironically, the extraterrestrial outsider would make outsiders of all humanity. The ideological prerogative to consider oneself a member of a specific country, for example, would seem silly. Citizens of one nation would no longer need to differentiate themselves from another. While a pessimist could argue that xenophobia is a part of human nature, that anxiety of the *other* would potentially turn from other humans to the radical alien other—an *exophobia* of sorts.

Beyond a potential dissolution of citizenship to a particular state (or perhaps the development of a "citizen of Earth" ideology) and government, so too would the human concept of the self be altered forever. The ideologies and illusions of what it means to be human would change insurmountably.

According to theorist Jodi Dean, this entire notion forces people to reassess their own identity. She writes, "the alien reassures us that *everything* is not up for grabs, but *anything* could be. Some things are certain. We just don't know what they are."[96]

Fundamentally, the perception of alien visitation, whether it is real or not, puts humanity into a conflict with itself. Fact and fiction are pushed to the edge when in contact with the *superior Other.* She writes:

---

[96] Dean, Jodi, 31.

The alien dares us to take a stand, to hold a position, to accept or reject it. Confrontation with a story of flying saucers or alien abduction pushes us to one side or another: Is it real? Do we believe? The alien seduces us into a critical reassessment of our criteria for truth: How do we determine what real is? Why do we believe? The claim to truth and its challenge to our practices for establishing it are what enable the alien to function as an icon of postmodern anxieties. Because its appeals to evidence incorporate scientific and juridical criteria, the alien works as an icon that allows us to link to embedded fears of invasion, violation, mutation. It uses the language of reality to contest our taken-for-granted experience of reality. The alien marks the radical strangeness and unknowability increasingly part of contemporary life. It serves as the ubiquitous reminder of uncertainty, doubt, suspicion, of the fugitivity of truth. We live with the alien while never knowing it.[97]

Similarly to Zimmerman, Dean's assessment is that the concept of the extraterrestrial forces an individual to make a choice, or perhaps removes the ability to choose altogether. The key position of the scientific and political cultures, in other words, the mainstream, is that aliens do not exist, at least not in any way that allows them to interact with humanity, because they would call into question the validity of those establishments. However, if a person comes to the table with an open mind and begins to consider that extraterrestrials may exist and are interacting with humanity, they are pulled into a battle with the self. Regardless of whether someone knows or believes that the Earth is being visited, that individual opens themselves up to a possible shift in perception: a sliver of doubt in the contemporary world order, in science and nationhood, in the illusion of mainstream ideology. To borrow a term from the philosopher Slavoj Zizek, they begin to *look awry* at the reality around them. It is all well and good to hypothesize that extraterrestrials may exist somewhere far away in the distant cosmos; however, to suggest that they are coming here is unthinkable.

Treading down this path puts humanity into contention with itself. The phantom of the self becomes lost in the gap between what it means to be human and alien. To look deeply into the UFO phenomenon, deconstructing the ideologies given us by the media or the charlatan ufological gurus who frequently lecture at UFO conferences, we realize

---

[97] Ibid.

that we are staring into a mirror. The extraterrestrial stands as a direct opposite to humanity, yet, totally "subverts us/them categories."[98]

That is not to say that humans and supposed aliens would be the same on a biological or materialist level; rather, if we are correct in saying that the extraterrestrial challenges our current paradigm of reality, and the zeitgeist of human social and cultural constructs, does it not then call into question the very nature of what it means to be human? Here the ghost appears again, throwing our assumptions into a disjointed middle ground. The UFO subculture, that group which has essentially climbed into this gap, or fallen into it, is in such a state—human and non-human, existing yet simultaneously not existing. Perhaps this is why the UFO community, the subculture, is so difficult to pin down, to be able clearly to ascertain who is a member and who is not.

As was pointed out earlier in this book, a subculture, by definition, requires some sort of dissenting ideology to separate it from the mainstream. Furthermore, it must act in some way that opposes the popular. While the extraterrestrial and the UFO constructs challenge our current ideological world view, these effects only matter when people (or aliens) get involved.

Cultural theorist Jodi Dean admits in her book that, like Harvard psychiatrist John Mack, her colleagues referred to her research into the UFO community as "white trash studies."[99] Dean points out that this elitist position is partially responsible for the allure of this field. She writes that:

> [the] stigma makes UFOs and alien abduction seductive, transgressive. Those of us attracted to left-wing causes, to critical positions against political, governmental, and corporate authorities, or maybe just to underdogs in general may feel at home in ufology.[100]

The UFO narrative is chock-full of stories that often target established power systems as being the enemy of truth. If we examine UFO literature, as well as the vast collection of websites, blogs, YouTube videos, and other discursive media that comes from the United States, much of it generally carries with it a tone of dissent. The UFO subculture has a certain feeling towards the government, the military-industrial

---

[98] Ibid.

[99] Dean, Jodi, 60.

[100] Ibid.

complex, and the establishments of authority, such as the corporate and scientific communities: that feeling is that they are not worthy of trust. Conspiracy theories, alleged whistleblowers, and leaked top secret documents all lend to this ideological build-up of opposition to elite power structures. Much of this opposition is misguided, conspiratorial, and even ridiculous. The "exopolitics" movement, Disclosure, the alien/Nazi "sekret machines" being worked on by Lockheed Martin Skunkworks, channeling alien communication, and ancient alien visitations are just a few examples that often fall into the trap of ideological nonsense and charlatanry. Inane or not, the consequence of these movements can be significant as they do alter the subcultural landscape, and, in turn, the landscape of the mainstream. Beyond this, there is a whole litany of radio shows, YouTube channels and podcasts that reinforce these ideologies; they repeat them, digitize them, and push them into the never-ending ether that is the Internet.

While certain aspects of government, or other powerful corporations and institutions, are perpetually under scrutiny from the UFO subculture, the "flavor of the week" changes so often that the dissenting ideology is essentially non-negotiable into mainstream culture. The constant shifting of who can and cannot be trusted is chaotic and seemingly follows no rhyme or reason. In simple terms, the tendrils of dissent move and spread so quickly in varying directions with no discernible pattern.

This all leads to a fundamental problem for mainstream power systems. This distrust of established social order has forced many members of the UFO subculture into a dual state: they function within that social order, but work against it ideologically, often unknowingly. The illusion of power is more important than the reality: if people cease to engage in the ideological illusion, then there is a major upheaval to the status quo. The upheaval will not necessarily destroy contemporary social systems, but may force them to undergo a significant adjustment, the most damaging of aspect of which is a shaking up of who wields control over power and knowledge.

The UFO community is, in essence, a "community in disconnect" rather than deviant. Its members are not "beholden to any nation nor offer their uncritical allegiance to the rhetoric of nationness or any such persuasion of belonging." [101] As John Mack pointed out in a lecture he gave at the International Association for New Science conference in 1995:

---

[101] Battaglia, 32.

> It is really going to be interesting to see when the official mainstream, the small percentage of elites that determine what we are supposed to think is real, wake up to the fact that the consensus view of reality is gone.

While many in UFO discourse view Disclosure, exopolitics or the channeling phenomenon as purely speculative, these are key examples of movements within UFO discourse that attempt to democratize power. While many disclosurists, "exopoliticians," and channellers are simple con-artists, the ideological perception of the phenomenon by the subculture generates a call of equality, free of established systems of governance or control. In essence, the Disclosure and exopolitics movements and the channelling phenomenon "promise" to reshape the world into one free of poverty, classism, nationalism, pollution and conflict. They attempt to create a worldview free of authoritative power and elitism. Mainstream ideologies fall into contention with a subculture that is attempting to envision an end to the mainstream itself. While the UFO subculture may never succeed, the consideration of such a reality is unacceptable, and, therefore, as most hardline skeptics will tell us, must be the musings of a sick and delusional mind.

Perhaps the most mind-boggling is that the subculture engages in such dissent without an established set of rules and without governance. There exists no hierarchy, domination, or subordination. It is a discourse with no locus of control, no elites, and no ivory tower that establishes *ideological truth*. There is no established power in the discourse, therefore power moves openly between constant shifts in ideas. The sciences, and any other academic or mainstream discourse, have visible establishments, which govern. They establish rules, hierarchies, and systems to control who is a member of the discourse, and what the discursive ideologies are. The UFO discourse has no such mechanism; it is an anarchy, with members of the subculture able to freely express their own ideologies, which vary from reasoned logic to utter malarkey. While this may be a key reason as to why ufology as a field of study has made little productive and objective progress, the discourse itself has functioned in this state since its inception, creating its own reality that does not require mainstream official ideologies in order to exist. In some perverse awareness, the collective mind of the UFO community understands that the status quo and the current power systems are present, but not permanent.

The UFO subculture is a community of renegades who make manifest the world view of the radical Other. To upset the social order, the alien is not even necessary. The UFO community can cause enough chaos on its own.

CHAPTER 16

Taboo

Sociologists Alexander Wendt and Raymond Duvall establish that UFOs are quantifiably a Derridean undecidable: Derrida's earlier linguistic philosophy, which forms the basis of his social and cultural theory concerning the ghost. UFOs are both object and subject. UFOs not only pose a problem to human anthropocentrism, as was pointed out earlier, but the subjective side of the undecided dualism creates a serious problem for people and governments as mentioned previously. For the sake of argument, if, due to their behavior, UFOs are piloted by an intelligent superior Other, that entity possesses some kind of will or agency.

Objectively, UFOs tend, occasionally, to leave trace evidence of their physical existence, such as blips on a radar screen, pieces of debris, depression marks signifying a landing, and being recorded on video. If that physical evidence is accurate and "real," UFOs do have some objective presence. Wendt and Duvall suggest that if UFOs were merely objective, then the matter would be simple: we can simply figure out what they are, like any other natural phenomenon, and move on with it.

This object/subject dichotomy removes the UFO from a singular state, and into the realm of the undecidable. It complicates the answer to the UFO question: if these anomalies are both objective and subjective, whatever physical evidence they leave behind must also possess the same undecidability. More importantly, it forces the hand of the general public, science, and the governments who maintain power to ensure the UFO question remains a question that no one with any authority wants to answer. Modern establishments, such as academia and government, and the scientists who answer to them, which nearly all—since very few scientists are free to study whatever they wish carte blanche—are essentially threatened by the dual nature of UFOs.

The study of UFOs would call into question the ideological constructs, which govern mainstream culture. Wendt and Duvall posit that this undecidability cannot compel an answer, as either side of the dualism would threaten human anthropocentrism. Instead, the authors suggest that the UFO object/subject is a "meta-undecidability." The UFO cannot, in effect, be decided upon, so it must enter another state: that of the taboo.

UFOs and those who study them are ridiculed because they must be; any seriousness given to the subject would compel a decision into their dualism, and, in turn, call into question human agency and any cultural institution, such as the general sciences, that rule over that agency.

~

While Wendt and Duvall provide an excellent exploration into the quantifiable undecidable dualism of the UFO as object, they do not go far enough to explore the cultural aspects of this undecidability. The nature of our cultural ideologies calls into question their assertion of human sovereignty, as well as the idea of anthropocentrism as an objective truth. The real answer to the UFO dualism lies within cultural reality and demands an exploration of *Truth* itself.

In official mainstream culture, UFOs do not exist because they cannot exist. To the general public, UFOs are not real because they are told they are not real. The ideologically constructed state of UFOs, fashioned by cultural institutions, is that they do not exist. However, people have reported seeing UFOs from far away and up close, being aboard them, and even meeting their pilots. To the UFO subculture, UFOs do exist. Since science has yet to establish with certainty that UFOs do not exist, and UFO believers have not been able to prove that they do, we are left in a quagmire of ideology. Scientists, stuck in their own paradigms, typically fall back upon the social construction known as "common sense" in regard to the UFO question, but possess no actual evidence to disprove their existence. While the onus may be on the UFO subculture to prove the existence of UFOs, for a scientist to state that UFOs (or extraterrestrials for that matter) do not exist is a scientific error. What occurs instead is a curious debate over which ideology is believed to be "truer."

The problem is that we cannot sort out which ideological "truth" is correct. The question manifests a phantom regarding *Truth* itself: official truth established by mainstream culture, media and scientific authority and "unofficial" truth generated by subversive social media, the UFO subculture and the lunatic fringe, and both exist simultaneously.

Typically we tie *Truth* to an objective reality. However, issues arise because we tend to place cultural interpretations upon that reality; we augment it with our perceptions, beliefs and values. The sciences attempt to provide a view into objective reality, but the fields of science are still bound by ideological constructs, such as nationalism, capitalism, and militarism to name a few. Furthermore, this age of insecurity that we live in only problematizes access to truth. It challenges us to *unknow* what we assume to be known.

Literary theorist and philosopher Colin Davis writes that:

> Derrida calls on us to endeavour to speak and listen to the specter, despite the reluctance inherited from our intellectual traditions and because of the challenge it may pose to them... Conversing with specters is not undertaken in the expectation that they will reveal some secret... Rather, it may open us up to the experience of secrecy as such: an essential unknowing, which underlies and may undermine what we think we know.[102]

It is incorrect to say that "science is wrong" and that the UFO subculture has some special access to a *higher truth*. The ghost is not necessarily honest, nor does it concern itself with what is true or not true; it bears out both.

Occasionally, the UFO phenomenon manifests in strange ways that can best be described as "absurd." So, too, UFO subculture has, at times, fallen off the slope and tumbled down quite quickly into absurdity. The UFO community is filled with salesmen, con artists, and enough people who are easily duped in order to buy the snake oil being sold. The mechanisms of capital and politics do drive ufology and the UFO subculture as much as they drive the sciences; the difference is that the sciences have much more to lose in the democratization of knowledge and power than the UFO subculture, which has everything to gain.

---

[102] Davis, Colin. "Hauntology, Specters and Phantoms." *French Studies*. Volume 59, Issue 3, 1 July 2005, 373–379. Found online at https://doi.org/10.1093/fs/kni143

The UFO subculture is not deviant because, much like the phenomenon itself, it shapes its own reality. It punches through the veil that we perceive as "normal" and into something else, some *otherness*, where official mainstream reality is powerless. The previous chapters have addressed the constant interplay of history and mythology; the cultural evolution of ideology concerning the UFO community and the extraterrestrial; and, finally, that the UFO subculture is a collection of outsiders because their ideologies do not challenge the formation and foundation of the status quo but deem them to be illusions and apparitions.

The result of engaging with the UFO on a cultural level creates anxiety on the part of the broader mainstream and official culture. By communing with the ghost, entering into the gaps between science and myth, object and subject, human and non-human, normal and paranormal, the UFO subculture itself becomes a ghost. The only option for the popular is to ward off the ghost in an attempt to send it away, place a taboo upon it, lest the ghost begins to dissolve the established social order. Ghosts, however, do not obey the rules. This cultural haunting by the UFO community is strengthened by its *subcultural geography*[103]

While many subcultures have a physical place, such as a city borough or certain hangout, contemporary technology has allowed for many subcultures to take up residency in the digital realm. The UFO community today primarily exists on the Internet. While there are conferences where members of the community gather, the vast majority of ufological discourse occurs on forums, blogs, social media, podcasts, and other digital mediums. Furthermore, much of the UFO subculture exists within this digital landscape by creating groups on Facebook or having debates on Reddit. The Internet has allowed for a democratization of knowledge output, and, while a significant amount of it is totally made up, it has opened the door to equalizing the voices of those in marginalized communities. The power of communication is not relegated to the elite few, but to all with a WiFi password.

Technology commentator and author Richard Thieme explains that the Internet does "obliterate historical sense" and that, due to a lack of reference, "all information seems equal."[104] When it comes to UFO information online, it is often reproduced, copies of copies, and

---

[103] Gelder, 4.

[104] Thieme, Richard. "Stalking the UFO Meme." CTHEORY Journal. 01/16/1997. http://ctheory.net/ctheory_wp/stalking-the-ufo-meme/

pushed around the globe. As Derrida points out, "time is out of joint." Ufological discourse, and the subculture itself, not only exists everywhere, but in all time as well. The subcultural ghost manifests the UFO phenomenon online all the time; its presence is eternal in the digital landscape, a virtual haunting, daring the bystander to engage with it.

Herein lies one of the key reasons why it is not the alien which is taboo, but the subculture itself. The influence of the subculture, its ability to move out from the realm of taboo, is limited only by how many people join a social media group or read a blog post. The more people who seek the specter, the more its influence grows. The effect that the subculture has upon mainstream culture by using the medium of the Internet has removed it from isolation. The established power systems, such as the scientific community, are unable to curb the growth of ufological discourse simply because the conditions of the Internet do not allow such control. Jodi Dean argues that:

> ... ufological discourse upholds the very criteria for scientific rationality that mainstream science uses to dismiss it. "Scientists" are the ones who have problems with the "rationality" of those in the UFO community. "Scientists" are the ones who feel a need to explain why some people believe in flying saucers, or who dismiss those who do so as "distorted" or "prejudiced" or "ignorant."[105]

As this continued attempt to control discourse on the part of science grows, so too does the mistrust in science, not in its ability to expand human understanding, but in the ideological power it wields. As the established systems of power attempt to advance upon the UFO debate, in the past, the UFO community would fall back and be warded off. Today, they simply hold their ground. Dean concludes:

> Those in positions of power deploy terms like "reasonable" and "rational." Previously, the victims of this deployment, the "unreasonable" and "irrational," remained isolated. They had difficulty getting attention and fighting back. Now, thanks to widespread developments in communication networks, the "irrational" can get their message out... they can reclaim their rationality on their own terms.[106]

---

[105] Dean, Jodi, 9.
[106] Ibid.

The ideological playing field is not even, but the medium of communication is. What has occurred is an outpouring of UFO discourse. Many UFO and paranormal Facebook groups, for example, number in the tens of thousands of members, with some near the one hundred thousand mark. YouTube videos of UFOs and alleged alien beings, hoaxed or not, have half a million views. The inherent issue for those in positions of power is that those numbers can increase. The *subcultural geography* of the UFO community is worldwide, everywhere digitally, but physically nowhere. The men and women who engage in the UFO debate are as elusive geographically as the UFOs they seek.

The common image that permeates popular discourse is that of the UFO fanatic hiding in a dark room in front of a computer screen. Most subcultures which have a significant Internet presence often are portrayed as anti-social deviants and loners by the mainstream media. However, this imagery is more fantasy than fact.[107] Rather, the development of "virtual communities" generates communication and a collective intelligence. What occurs is a socialization and sharing of ideas. The digital landscape has also created a subculture devoid of a set leadership or social order. There is no ivory tower of UFO discourse, and no one person or group is the face of the UFO debate. Rather, what exists is a total democracy, if not anarchy, within the community. This chaotic state is empowering but also destructive. While it empowers members of the community to share their theories and hypotheses, it also generates significant useless ideological noise whereupon the signal often becomes lost.

It becomes impossible to separate the valid from the nonsense, the useful information concerning the phenomenon and the ravings of zealots, charlatans and knee-jerk debunkers. To the mainstream, particularly those who are critical of the UFO community, this chaotic state is a sign of a troubled future. In an age where "fake news" and "alternative facts" are buzzwords, the UFO community's inability to maintain a semblance of order over its ideologies is another nail in the coffin of rational thinking and logic. Be that as it may, it speaks to Jodi Dean's argument, above, concerning power and rationality. Like it or not, consensus reality, and what is considered rational by the mainstream, changes. Change is not the issue, rather, it is the *who* that is behind that change. Significant anxiety exists concerning the UFO subculture that one day there may be enough ideological power to tip

---

[107] Gelder, 147.

the scales. The Internet gives voice to all, even those not in the popular majority. Those on the cultural interior, who control popular discursive paradigms, may find themselves pushed to the outer fringes, or, worse, realize that they always have been teetering on the edge and the slightest change may send them over the precipice.

CHAPTER 17

Exoculture

If we are willing to believe, even if only for a moment, that a visiting *Other* is more than delusion or story. If we are willing to say that maybe, just maybe, UFOs do exist and that some intelligent Other is interacting with humanity on some level, then we establish a perceived reality. UFO researcher and writer Miguel Romero sums this up with a simple statement: "If UFOs are "real," then we don't actually understand what 'Reality' is."[108]

It is not that the extraterrestrial or UFO deviates from the mainstream, from the normal, rather, it creates its own reality, its own version of what is normal. The very possibility that the UFO phenomenon is objectively real does not simply oppose human anthropocentrism or sovereignty, it replaces it. It generates a new version of the real: a reality where humanity can no longer rely on common sense or consensus. The entire landscape of "common" and "consensus" shifts; it falls out right underneath our perceptions of the normal, and launches, not into the paranormal, but something totally unknown.

I have argued in the book, thus far, that the UFO subculture does not have a common identity or style but is so varied that one cannot delineate its place and people. Nor can the subculture be deviant, because that assumes mainstream ideology is somehow established to be objectively "true." In other words, the UFO subculture recognizes that

---

[108] Personal correspondence. October 2017.

deviance is not possible when the ideologies from which it deviates are arbitrary and illusory. Much like the ghost, it is uncontrollable, unknowable, and unfathomable because the UFO subculture exists and does not exist simultaneously, nor does it recognize the consensus formed by official and mainstream culture. It is both fact and fiction, truth and myth, familiar and stranger, human and alien. It is not that the UFO subculture *believes in some radical Other; it is the radical Other.*

The philosopher Ludwig Wittgenstein proposed a famous thought experiment known as "the beetle in the box." It goes like this. Suppose that everyone carried around with them a box with something inside it; that something we all call a "beetle." No one is allowed to look inside anyone else's box, and everyone says they know what a "beetle" is simply by looking at their own "beetle." As Wittgenstein sums up, "here it would be quite possible for everyone to have something different in his box."[109]

His intention was to point out the inherent problem in language, and, by extension, the experience of the individual. We can only speak to our own experiences and ideas via language. The words are not the problem, rather, it is the fact that we have only our own understanding of those experiences and ideas, and, as Derrida teaches us, language is very complicated in its ability to shift meaning. We all have boxes. We all have something inside our box that we can talk about. The problem is that I can only talk to you about the stuff inside your box based upon what's in mine. There exists a significant gap within experience: the subjective personal experience and the general understanding of it by others. Furthermore, what lies in the gap between personal introspection of a concept, or how I know that thing, versus how do others know and interpret that thing?

He writes, "if we construe the grammar of the expression of sensation on the model of 'object and designation' the object drops out of consideration as irrelevant."[110]

In other words, the actual thing inside the box, the beetle, is irrelevant. What matters is how the idea of the beetle is communicated to others. We can all talk about beetles, yet we have no idea if our beetle looks or is like anyone else's. Complicate this now with how we experience the world around us. I can tell you about my subjective experiences, but you must use your own subjective experiences to understand mine.

---

[109] Wittgenstein, Ludwig. *Philosophical Investigations.* Basil Blackwell pub. 1954, 293.

[110] Ibid.

The subculture is able to communicate about UFOs and aliens—their beetles—however, we cannot gain objective access to the UFO reality. No one knows what is truly in the various boxes held. The beetle, then, as object, as meaning, as ghost, exists and does not exist. While one could argue, ultimately, that perhaps the boxes are empty, every experience will have a source; the beetle, or something anyway, is crawling around in the box as we can feel it shake in our hand. The ghost manifests, even if we do not understand how. If I experience the UFO, the alien, or generate a discourse concerning it, only I can establish and "truly know" its reality unto myself.

All this brings us to a curious place: a place where the UFO, and all paranormal phenomena, are both real, objective, and imaginary, subjective. Perhaps these phenomena come from Corbin's realm of *the mundis imaginalis?* This place is a gap between worlds, where the binary oppositions between real and unreal, reality and myth, collapse. Where "reality, the imaginal, and fantasy blur into one another." [111] It is not that UFOs are actual objects flying in the sky. Nor is it that they are pure imagination and fantasy. They are both.

In other words, people will have to open their own boxes to sort out what that discourse means to them. Something is fundamentally in the box; it can be debated over and talked about, but its objective and collective meaning, its 'truth' is not always derived from objectivity, but from the discussion, from speaking of it or mythologizing it. In other words, the UFO and the extraterrestrial are irrelevant—the discourse is all that matters.

Author George Hansen's work concerning paranormal phenomena focused on the trickster archetype. However, we could easily replace Derrida's ghost with the trickster, as, at times, they function very similarly. He writes:

> The trickster is not eliminated simply by making sharp distinctions and clear categories. There is still a realm that lies betwixt and between a signifier and signified, between a word and its referent. Tricksters travel that liminal realm, and ambiguities in communication are their province.[112]

---

[111] Hansen, George P. *The Trickster and the Paranormal.* Kindle Locations 7489-7490. Xlibris US. Kindle Edition.

[112] Ibid (Loc. 413).

Here is the inherent reason why the UFO subculture is truly alien. For the conversation to continue and to thrive, there doesn't necessarily need to be a UFO or an extraterrestrial from another physical planet. To paraphrase Shakespeare's *A Midsummer's Night's Dream*, perhaps it is the subculture itself, which "turns them to shapes and gives to airy nothing a local habitation and a name." Or, perhaps the source of the UFO phenomenon construes its own meaning from the subculture like a sounding board. Whatever the case, the UFO subculture functions easily in the gap between objective and subjective and continues to push the boundaries of rational thought. The UFO subculture itself is Derrida's ghost. It dwells in the margins and gaps, but it also transgresses them—an outsider to what everyone else considers inside.

To borrow a term from psychology, the phenomenon itself is *uncanny*. As anthropologist and researcher Susan Lepselter suggests, "Thinking through the uncanny heightens my sense of 'something more.'"[113] The UFO, as object, rubs up against normality, pushes it, alters it, and establishes an unfamiliar reality within a common frame of reference. It "unifies story fragments... and then ruptures them again. On the one hand, it strains towards rupture; on the other, it works through an obsessive attention to structure."

There is a sense of encroachment, a *them* hiding amongst the *us*. While the phenomenon often has shadows of the uncanny, the subculture itself is often patterned in this way. The community seeks to establish the UFO as reality, measurable, objective and scientific, yet, in the same breath, ruptures that narrative, calling out the very science it is trying to use as being broken, dogmatic and limited in its scope to imagine something beyond itself. The UFO community wants to be adopted by official culture, given a home within it, yet simultaneously works to undermine and question officialdom and the mainstream.

Coming to terms with the arbitrariness of official culture is similar to being abducted by aliens. Jodi Dean writes:

> Our agency was an illusion, just like our security and certainty... the alien... reminds us that nothing is completely other (and everything is somewhat other), that the very border between 'like' and 'unlike' is illusory.[114]

---

[113] Lepselter, Susan. The License: Poetics, Power and The Uncanny, in: *E.T. Culture: Anthropology in Outerspaces*. Duke University Press. 2005, 141.

[114] Dean. 1998, 174-175.

Dean points out that normalcy is nothing more than an illusion. The extraterrestrial, as a cultural construct, and the subculture as the purveyor of that construct, force us to concede that.

Jeffrey Kripal suggests that the UFO phenomenon is more than mere materialism. He writes:

> Although paranormal phenomena certainly involve material processes, they are finally organized around signs and meaning. To use the technical terms, they are semiotic and hermeneutical phenomena. Which is to say that they seem to function as representations or signs to decipher and interpret, not just movements of matter to measure and quantify.... paranormal phenomena are semiotic or hermeneutical phenomena in the sense that they signal, symbolize, or speak across a "gap" between the conscious, socialized ego and an unconscious or superconscious field. It is this gap between two orders of consciousness... that demands interpretation and makes any attempt to interpret such events literally look foolish and silly. We thus ignore this gap and the call to interpret signs across different orders of consciousness at great peril.[115]

One cannot fully comprehend the UFO; similarly, one cannot comprehend the subculture, which generates the reality for that UFO to manifest. This "gap" is where the UFO community lives, a state between everywhere and nowhere. The true ghost in regard to UFO discourse is not the UFO or the alien: it is the subculture itself. It consumes and creates symbolic meaning and, in turn, interprets it, making it real in some sense. To put it another way, it is not the UFO phenomenon which draws together the people who make up the UFO subculture, rather, it is the gap itself. It is the strange world between object and subject, where official and mainstream culture ceases to exist, and, in turn, the reality created is something truly unknown, something fundamentally and totally alien.

One can never truly know *what* the UFO subculture is because it reshapes our ideas of what subculture itself is. It is an oxymoron, an impossibility, yet it exists. Not only is it an outsider to broader culture, it is also an outsider to itself. No other subculture exists in such a phantasmal state.

Just as the extraterrestrial challenges established anthropocentric ideologies, the UFO subculture *others* the mainstream and the truths

---

[115] Kripal pp. 25

it attempts to assert. It asserts that the popular zeitgeist is false, and that consensus reality is an illusion, another ghost perhaps, and truly alien in every way. The subculture makes outsiders of all of humanity; it exposes the reality that we take for granted as being arbitrary, and the institutions of our society as ghosts themselves. It is not that UFOs or aliens are illusions, but rather, our daily lives are.

The UFO narrative is full of stories concerning aliens, aliens who, according to official culture, cannot exist, therefore they do not exist. Similarly, the UFO community does not exist because it cannot. However, here we are. Watching from the outside, and the inside, both alien and familiar, reminding the mainstream that there is precious little difference between the two sides of the curtain. The subculture, whether intentionally or not, places itself outside of the popular zeitgeist, and, furthermore, challenges that zeitgeist by holding up a mirror. The UFO community and the ideologies that it generates exposes the arbitrary illusions of the mainstream propped up by contemporary power systems, primarily that of science and capital.

The UFO community is ideologically free from the constraints of a popular world view. It is ever present and ever evolving, never attaching itself to one ideology for too long before cracks and splinters arise to shift the discourse. It is a perfectly functioning anarchy let loose upon a global communication network advancing slowly upon popular discourse. It has no leadership or allegiance, no system by which the mainstream can appropriate it or destroy it. It has no objective established culture of its own. It is a totally alien culture, extraterrestrial in nature, a sovereign collective, a 'meta-subculture', a ghost, or perhaps more appropriately, an *exoculture*, which ideologically resides simultaneously within what is considered normal and paranormal, known and unknown.

The UFO phenomenon and discourse, in truth, is not about alien hybrid breeding programs, Reptilian bases on the Moon, or an attempt to warn humanity about nuclear weapons, global warming or raising the vibration level of the planet. It is not about CE-5 meditation, trans-dimensional portals, paranormal ranches in Utah, or secret Deep State cabals. Nor is it about time traveling soldiers sent to fight on Mars, channeling Pleadian aliens, EBEs from Zeta Reticuli, Area 51, Element 115, or pulling little bits of metal out of abductees. These, and the rest of the myths within the UFO narrative, are ghost stories, which speak to our current place within the cultural illusion. They are cultural artifacts, constructs, which exist because of our current ideological framework. They will change because the symbolic systems, which they stem from, will change. This is does not mean that they are not true or real in some way. *I don't know.* Perhaps the source of the phenomenon is haunting us in some way, using our ghost stories to give itself place and form. What is certain, however, is that they are illusions and myths, which will evolve.

Addressing that the illusion exists is uncomfortable, but necessary. The UFO discourse is an impressive collection of spells, magic and story. It creates a foundation of lore and mythology based upon the fears and desires of humanity, the most startling of which is that absolutely nothing is certain.

It is not that UFOs do not exist, and it is not that thousands upon thousands of people are delusional or lying about their experiences. There is something happening, something strange and anomalous; it manifests all over the world, and it is something that potentially exists both inside and outside of the human frame of reference. The only place one can begin, and end is with an *"I don't know."* The UFO subculture is, in essence, a community that exists in the gap of not knowing. More importantly, it alerts the mainstream public that they do not know either. This grasp we have upon knowledge and our world is tenuous at best. This is why the UFO subculture is not allowed to participate in the serious worlds of academics or science; it challenges the very methods by which we engage with reality itself. We all become *the Other.*

Those who make claims to know the truth about UFOs and the paranormal in general are false idols, pillars of the ideological illusion, who attempt to root the UFO phenomenon in their own personal self-serving version of reality. Seeking ideological or spiritual refuge in the UFO experts, gurus, alien channelers, healers, and New Age messiahs is simply staring into the eyes of the Wizard of Oz. He demands your attention with booming voice and splendor, and it all just seems so true and magnificent. That is until you look behind the curtain, and you see the source of the illusion.

We must be cautious. The *UFO exoculture* is not some source of truth. Seeking answers in it is no different than assuming reality is driven by the mainstream and the popular, by science, or by some form of arbitrary consensus. It is not that the UFO community has access to some higher knowledge or true reality. It, too, is a source of illusion; it, too, is a collection of ghosts who haunt and inspire strange tales to be told around the campfire.

The phenomenon does not bring with it some objective truth, nor some unadulterated interpretation of *the real.* Rather, it seems that the role of the UFO and the extraterrestrial is to generate anxiety. Just as the UFO and the extraterrestrial cause anxiety for the witness, so, too, must the *exoculture* cause anxiety for the popular and the status quo. The anxiety of the *I don't know*, the anxiety one feels when being haunted by a specter, living in a state without definition; knowing that there is a curtain which must be lifted but knowing full well that the very act will change everything. It is not that truth or objectivity is relative, it is merely that our every attempt to seek it out makes it so. Professor Jeffrey Kripal sums up that "...the point is not to adopt this or that symbolic system as somehow literally true. The point is to be simultaneously sympathetic to and suspicious of all symbolic systems..."[116]

Perhaps it isn't the *UFO exoculture* which exists at the cultural fringe because, much like the construct of the visiting extraterrestrial, that radical *Other*, and the ghost, it disassembles our assumed realities. Rather, there is no fringe.

As Vallée questions: "Are the UFOs 'windows' rather than 'objects'?"[117]

For the UFO community, they are windows which open into a strange new world filled to the brim with possibilities, where the ideological differences between familiar and strange unravel. Indeed, real alienation rests in setting things in stone.

It is not that the UFO community is special or unique, and it is not the case that their viewpoint is true or even better. The varied stories of witnesses, some of which are absurd, and the supposed disinformation generated by the intelligence community, only proves that the UFO community must be at home in the *I don't know*, and, from there, they strike out with ideas that reshape all of reality. In all of this, though, they are still lost, stranded like the pilot of a crashed flying saucer, in a world where official and mainstream ideology generate this complex illusion, which all of us dwell in day to day.

I am reminded of Whitley Strieber' famous book, *Communion*. Strieber questions the often-traumatic actions of his alien abductors by telling them, "You have no right."[118]

Extraterrestrials and UFOs in the mythological narrative do not comply with human political, ethical or ideological boundaries, and neither does the subculture. Much like the alien and the ghost, the subculture deems consensus reality moot. The mainstream attempts to

---

[116] Kripal. Pp.

[117] Vallée, 156.

[118] Streiber, Whitley. *Communion*. Arrow Books: UK. 1987. 107

force the UFO community into a fringe cultural space, claiming that the subculture has no right to challenge the status quo. The fundamental misunderstanding on the part of the popular, much like Strieber himself, is that it does not fully comprehend the scope of the situation. As with any phantom, it does not haunt because of duty or some moral obligation; so, too, with the subculture, it does not exist because it is "better" or "honest." It simply is. The specter haunts, not because it should, but because that is all it can do. It has every right to be itself, causing anxiety and throwing our perception of what is real and what is not into the trash. Strieber's alien beings answer him with a simple and chilling response, which encapsulates their position, and, indeed, the position of the UFO subculture which communes with official culture, "We do have a right."[119]

The people who make up this curious *exoculture*, those who thrive in the *I don't know*, not the zealots, truthers, or debunkers, but the true outsiders, the ones who fell to Earth, do not view this phenomenon, nor the world, in absolutes. The lines between fact and fiction, known and unknown, human and non-human are not fixed but in a state of constant transference. The UFO, that elusive phantom, which they hunt, has made ghosts of us all. The UFO subculture's ever evolving reality, their *terra obscura*, begs a simple question of the mainstream: *if we are outsiders, what does that make you?*

---

[119] Ibid.

EPILOGUE

In November of 2017, during my research for this book, I was told the following story.

The great Sufi master Mullah Nasruddin was on his hands and knees searching for something under a streetlamp. A man saw him and asked,
"What are you looking for?"
"My house key," Nasruddin replied. "I lost it."
The man joined him in looking for the key, and after a period of fruitless searching, the man asked, "Are you sure you lost it around here?"
Nasruddin replied, "Oh, I didn't lose it around here. I lost it over there, by my house."
"Then why," the man asked, "are you looking for it over here?"
"Because," Nasruddin said, "The light is so much better over here."

The UFO subculture is looking for the key but applies to their search all the paradigms and ideologies which come, not from UFOs or alien entities, but from themselves. It is easier to look where we are comfortable and where we can see.

Perhaps looking for the key in the darkness away from the streetlamp is impossible, and perhaps the answer, whatever it may be, will never come. Or, maybe someday, a few honest passers-by will just trip over that key in the dark and bring it to all of us who are stumbling about looking for something that isn't there.

The UFO enigma, real and not real, factual and fictional, matters. Moreover, significantly more work needs to be done to understand its implications upon us. In infinitely small measures, the UFO enigma affects our cultures, our societies, and us. Mythology, no matter how wild or absurd, generates our reality. We are all haunted by the very idea of the UFO, as friend and foe, as technological and spiritual savior, and as destructive invader.

Appreciating the ghostly nature of the phenomenon, by applying philosophy and theory to it, we can begin to pick apart the ideologies and illusions, which we've built around it. When we begin to understand that some of the most basic yet prolific building blocks of the ufological and paranormal narratives are simply constructs that we've built, we can begin to look critically at them. We can try to peel them away and grow beyond them, however, always aware that as we grow, and as we develop new understandings, we will continue, inadvertently, to add more layers. Once we recognize that the UFO phenomenon is separate from us and also a part of us, only then will we make any progress.

Amy, with her many encounters on her quiet farm, has transcended the illusion and entered into another place. What that place is, I cannot say. Perhaps it is another illusion or perhaps something more real than you or I can possibly imagine. I hope that she will learn her place in this mystery. To her, to all those researchers and seekers, and to all the UFO people, may you find your key in the darkness.

CATHERINE CROWE AND THE LONG ROAD TO PARANORMAL EQUALITY

By Allison Jornlin

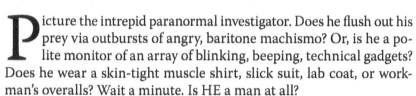

Picture the intrepid paranormal investigator. Does he flush out his prey via outbursts of angry, baritone machismo? Or, is he a polite monitor of an array of blinking, beeping, technical gadgets? Does he wear a skin-tight muscle shirt, slick suit, lab coat, or workman's overalls? Wait a minute. Is HE a man at all?

If you've glimpsed even a wee bit of paranormal TV over the last, say, 20 years, you've beheld a screen-scape overrun with spooky dudes of all varieties and few women, and most of them cast into the accepted, but limited roles of "psychic" or "witch" or "medium". If you happen to be female, investigator status in Reality Television, at least, is, to-date, only bestowed regularly upon applicants nubile enough to appear on TV. No crones or dowagers need apply. But is this an accurate depiction of the ghost hunting field in general, parapsychology in particular, or even the history of paranormal investigation? Nope; not at all. Reality TV, although it currently seems to be the dominant organ of societal perception and expression, is not an accurate depiction of real life. In fact, in the case of paranormal investigation and its unquestioned portrayal of male primacy in the field, Reality TV is about as far away from the truth as you can get.

The original paranormal investigator was, in fact, a woman. Catherine Crowe (1790-1872) could be called the mother of modern parapsychological studies. There were no doubt others before her who were interested in strange phenomena and even those who put together collections of true ghost stories, but Crowe went way beyond merely collecting tales. Early 20th Century ghost hunter Harry Price refers to her work as simply a compilation of "possible and impossible ghost stories" and still others refer to it as nothing more than an assortment of paranormal gossip. However, these judgements say more about the critics than the content as perhaps our failure to recognize Crowe's contributions says more about us, and our limited knowledge of the history of paranormal investigation, than we might like.

Even a casual reading reveals that Crowe's scope rockets past simple ghost stories to include tales, which clearly don't fit that mold. Crowe carefully examined those accounts that don't follow the familiar narrative and provided some of the earliest recognition of a variety of unexplained phenomena including what we now call OBEs, NDEs, time slips, ESP, etc. Her purpose was that of a scientist—identification, delineation, and classification. Crowe sought a taxonomy of the unexplained to foster a greater understanding of relationships and ultimately to get us closer to what is really going on.

A close reading of Crowe reveals a meta-analysis of early studies in the field of what was to become parapsychological research. In fact, she leads us to question the nature of reality itself. Crowe was clearly far ahead of her time, so why have other researchers been so dismissive of her or, worse, failed to mention her work at all? Are they envious because she got there first? Indeed, her ground-breaking research is still relevant today. In fact, it is not an exaggeration to say that Catherine Crowe has influenced every single one of us in today's paranormal arena; we just don't know it yet.

Crowe compiled and compared cross-cultural data about a wide variety of strange phenomena.

She was one of those rare multilingual researchers who scoured the literature of non-English speaking countries for anomalies. Inspired by German scholars in particular, Crowe brought the ideas of leading physicians, physiologists, and other scientists, including Justinus

Kerner and others too numerous to mention, to English-speaking readers.

You're familiar with the words "poltergeist" and "doppelgänger" because she introduced the terms and concepts to English usage. Crowe also investigated hauntings in a manner we would still recognize today. In 1854, for example, she organized a party of witnesses to investigate a notorious haunted house in Edinburgh. She enlisted a clairvoyant and several esteemed members of the community to make contact with the spirits of those murdered on the premises and dutifully recorded their experiences. Crowe and the clairvoyant observed "waves of white light" emanating from the floor in intervals. Crowe and another witness glimpsed "a bright diamond of light, white brilliant and quiescent". This paranormal investigation led by Crowe is likely the first of its kind.

Catherine Crowe penned *The Night-Side of Nature. Or, Ghosts and Ghost Seers* in 1848, a time when women didn't have the right to vote or own property or do much of anything on their own. Nevertheless, Crowe persisted. She became an independent woman, living in Edinburgh, who left London and her husband to pursue her dream of becoming a writer. Challenging convention she interviewed witnesses, pioneered paranormal investigation techniques, and investigated séance circles decades before Harry Houdini was even born. *The Night-Side of Nature*, published just as the Spiritualist movement was getting underway, rocketed Crowe to fame. *Night-Side* blazed a trail with 16 editions in just six years.

Catherine Crowe had a message for the world for which she used every means in her power to convey. She was inspired to do her own investigations of strange phenomena after much reading on the topic and translating one such work called *The Seeress of Prevorst* in 1845. The book was written by well-respected German physician Justinus Kerner as a case history of his extraordinary patient Friederike Hauffe. Hauffe was a medium who spent most of her life in trance states overcome with prophetic dreams and visions of spirit communication. *The Night-Side of Nature* was meant to foster the budding field of psychical research by providing a categorical record of dreams, presentiments, warnings, trances, wraiths, apparitions, spectral lights, haunted houses, poltergeists, and other revelations, together with an appeal for the serious scientific investigation of all such phenomena. In 1859, Crowe would also publish two other volumes devoted to paranormal study, *Ghosts and Family Legends and Spiritualism*, and *The Age We Live In*.

Known as "the ghost-fancier" to some and described by one magazine of the day as a fearless explorer who pitches her tent "in that shadowy borderland which separates the things which are seen and temporal from the things which are unseen and eternal." She set out to examine every known form of psychic phenomena and, in doing so, defined many of the mysteries with which modern-day investigators still grapple.

We can get a sense of Catherine Crowe from what others have written about her. Author of *The Constitution of Man*, one of the most influential rationalist books of the 19th Century, George Combe was a close friend of Catherine Crowe. Combe credited Crowe's lust for adventure to "a most preposterous organ of wonder". Writer and paranormal researcher Colin Wilson called *The Night-Side of Nature* "the first sustained attempt to treat paranormal phenomena in the scientific spirit that would later characterize the Society of Psychical Research." Almost 35 years after its publication, the SPR would continue Crowe's work by adopting many of her methods.

"We have an indefeasible right to investigate every question that presents itself to our intellects; and it is not only a right, but an urgent duty, to investigate one that so nearly concerns our well-being here and hereafter," Crowe writes. However, she condemned "pharisaical skepticism which denies without investigation" and "blind credulity which accepts all . . . without inquiry."

She was searching for an objective approach to paranormal investigation and was able to identify and distinguish between many unexplained phenomena, which investigators are still studying today. Many findings commonly misattributed to contemporary researchers can be found in Crowe's writing.

For example, Crowe has a surprisingly modern-sounding take on poltergeist phenomena. If Crowe is known at all, she is most often just credited with introducing the term poltergeist into English, but she hypothesized about them a great deal looking for possible causes. Poltergeists ("racketing specter" in German), she says, can scarcely be reconciled to our typical notions of "what we understand by the term 'ghost'" due to the "odd, sportive, mischievous nature of the disturbances". Crowe maintains that these nonsensical incursions into normal reality have been reported in all countries and all ages. Although, throughout the centuries, poltergeist activity has been ascribed to many different causes including ghosts, witchcraft, demons, and fairies, Crowe ascribes them most often to a human agent. In the 20th Century, parapsychologists Nandor Fodor and William G. Roll suggested that poltergeist activity might be caused by psychokinesis, however Crowe proposed something similar in 1848.

In *The Night Side of Nature*, she relates several cases of teen girls who have been beset with wild talents that include the ability to deliver electric shocks, in one recorded instance, even remotely and purposefully. One such human agent of this strange phenomenon was a young lady living in Strasberg, Germany, identified only by the surname Emmerich. Crowe relates that "her body became so surcharged with electricity, that it was necessary to her relief to discharge it". Unfortunately, this strange malady soon claimed her life. Crowe speculates that these strange circumstances may be connected to some form of electricity or displaced energy. "We begin to see that it is just possible the other strange phenomena [related to poltergeist activity] may be provided by a similar agency."

However, Crowe recounts other poltergeist phenomena, which might have a different explanation. Although in most cases the activity can be attributed to one person, sometimes it cannot. For these instances, she proposes an idea that seems to be straight out of John Keel's *The Mothman Prophecies*. Crowe challenges the reader to view human beings as just one class "in an immense range of existences." "Do not these strange occurrences suggest . . . that occasionally some individual out of this gamut of beings comes into rapport with us, or crosses our path like a comet," Crowe asks. "While certain conditions last, [perhaps such a strange being] can hover about us, and play these puckish, mischievous tricks, till the charm is broken, and then it re-enters its own sphere, and we are cognizant of it no more!"

In another poltergeist case, in which a man is followed everywhere for most of his life by a home-wrecking spirit that often leaves him lonely, jobless, and homeless, Crowe surmises that perhaps some invisible tormentor oppresses the victim through an unseen attachment. Her attention inevitably turned, then, to cases of possession in which spirits of the dead and, perhaps, sometimes something demonic, take control of the bodies of the living. Crowe's prescription is surprisingly secular for the time or even today. She describes no cases where the Roman Rite is performed as one might expect. Instead she reveals several instances where mesmerism, what we know today as hypnosis, was used successfully to cure the afflicted.

Crowe also introduced the term "doppelgänger" into the English language, although the identical concept of the fetch, or look-alike harbinger of imminent death, was alive and well in the British Isles. Even Frankenstein author Mary Shelley's husband, Percy, along with another independent witness, reportedly saw his double only days before his death at sea. Crowe, of course, relates tales of this folkloric portent of doom, but she also presents those reports that don't match that tradition. Some of these accounts more closely resemble the vardøger, or spirit predecessor of Norse mythology, the hallmark of this double is much less sinister; it just arrives before you do and gets on with your work until you actually arrive.

Crowe considers such harmless doubles a form of bilocation, where the thoughts of a person who is very anxious to arrive somehow propel their spirit forward. The Germans were already calling it "out of body" travel, according to Crowe. One exemplary tale concerned a minister named Joseph Wilkins who dreamt he visited his parents' house. He startled his mother who was sitting up in a chair. She immediately wrote him to make sure he was still alive and, in doing so, confirmed all the circumstances he had perceived in what he had mistook for just a dream. Crowe says of the phenomenon, "a spirit out of the flesh . . . must be where its thoughts and affections are, for its thought and affections are itself." Crowe also presents tales of anxious witnesses who report seeing a faraway loved one who visits in spirit form as if to say one final farewell at the moment of death. Such a common phenomenon, later dubbed the crisis apparition, was studied extensively just a few decades later in the book *Phantasms of the Living* published in 1886 by the Society for Psychical Research.

Crowe also shares what may be the first documented near-death experience, recorded by Plutarch 2,000 years before Raymond Moody coined the term in 1975. A man named Thespesius fell from a great height and, once revived, transformed from a "vicious reprobate" to the "most virtuous of men." When questioned, he said he had been afloat in "a sea of light."

Much of Crowe's work resonates even today. Orbs, shadow people, time slips, twin telepathy, and every variety of precognition all feature prominently in her writing. The anecdotal evidence, which Crowe collected for nearly every type of strange phenomenon, laid important groundwork. Fortunately, others, like the researchers of the Society for Psychical Research, followed in her footsteps and began accumulating the necessary data to build a stronger foundation for the future discoveries. Crowe's primary objective was "to induce a few capable persons, instead of laughing at these things, to look at them."

All science begins as speculative philosophy and is pushed forward by theorists, and then experimenters, as they devise the methodology to drag us all into a deeper understanding. Ultimately the knowledge is passed on to technicians who may use it every day but have no idea or appreciation of where the creative spark, the very basis of their occupation, originated.

There is a profound question that remains. Do we in the paranormal field really want to foster a society where the popular persona of so-called researchers is more revered for emulating a superficial, overly-aggressive hunk of muscle than a thoughtful, trailblazing, polyglot? If so, it seems that Western culture has regressed, taking parapsychology with it. It was Crowe's hope that "what is true lives . . . and what is false dies and is forgotten." Is the state of the field today just the opposite?

Unfortunately, most of us have completely forgotten Crowe and her contributions to the psychical research community. Crowe made ground-breaking contributions to paranormal study and it's time to give credit where it is due. It's time to remember those long forgotten, lest we lose what there is to be learned from their efforts.

No portrait of Catherine Crowe exists, just the faintest, pencil sketch of her face. Perhaps this is a profound message for us today because why should it matter what she looked like? Doesn't the quality of an investigator's work, male or female, stand on its own? If that's what we, as paranormal investigators, really believe, let's start acting like it. Let's revere those who have done the work and add their findings to the prerequisite cannon of parapsychological literature instead of rallying around a TV cult of personality that does little to advance the field.

The deeper message, here, is to avoid taking anything at face-value. "My object," Crowe explained, "is to suggest inquiry and stimulate observation, in order that we may endeavor, if possible, to discover something regarding our psychical nature, as it exists here in the flesh, and as it is to exist hereafter, out of it." Catherine Crowe looked closer, peering deep beneath the surface to uncover what mysteries await there for all of us and now, from beyond the grave, she urges you to do the same.

APPENDIX B

THE EVOLUTION OF THE EXTRATERRESTRAIL HYPOTHESIS WITHIN THE UFO SUBCULTURE: AN OPINION

By Barry Greenwood and Paul Dean

UFOs have been present throughout much of man's recorded history. That is not to say that aliens have visited Earth in that time but the term "UFO" is being used in the strictest sense, meaning *"unidentified* flying objects." Reports of "flying shields," "flying ships," and "flying torches" can be found in Roman literature, baffling witnesses who noted such details within their minds' eye and context of the time. Later, "flying wash basins," strange dark globes in the sky and bodies crossing in front of the sun had been reported in the middle ages. Odd bodies in the sky can be found in paintings and broadsheets during the 15th and 16th centuries, notable examples being a 16th-century woodcut by Samuel Coccius (Samuel Koch) and Samuel Apiarius; a September 1609 report from the then Kingdom of Joseon in present day South Korea of a flying "bowl" that maneuvered in the sky, attempted to land and took off again in a shower of sparks, and the 1486 painting "Annunciation with Saint Emidus" by Carlo Crivelli of a miraculous halo.[120] Once again, these perceived, strange, aerial objects are described in the eye of the beholder, using what was common to the culture of the time in the form of religious images, bowls, shields. In a majority of instances, the apparitions were ascribed to the machinations of the gods' making themselves known to the world through seemingly heavenly displays. The persistence of odd, aerial sightings continued into the 18th and 19th centuries. Ballooning had become the first means of man's being able to engage in flight using a form of airborne vehicle with simple hot air as power. The beginnings of the industrial revolution, and of aerial travel created by man, inspired people on the ground to think about and observe the sky in ever-increasing detail. When general literature of those times is examined, one can see the change in language and the transmission of information from a literary, flowery form of description to a more concise, technical means of informing the reading public, paralleling the need to understand the rise of technology and to use the fruits of invention being developed. Aerial vehicles were becoming a goal to conquer the sky and to exploit the many new uses evident that aircraft could fulfill: quicker transportation for government, business and people simply hungry for new adventures.

~

Through the 19th century, there seemed to be an increasing trend of reports of aerial phenomena. Some were well understood but remained visual marvels as with rainbows and other common mirage displays. Some were not well understood but eventually became clearer to later generations as with infrequent weather oddities like tornadoes, rare mirage displays, falls of frogs, and lightning phenomena, such as sprites and jets, only recently understood. Then there were some events that were, and are, difficult to explain and continue to puzzle. Author William Corliss[121] created a series of books organizing and cataloguing a wide array of interesting events dating well into the past. Many are

---

[120] See for example: https://en.wikipedia.org/wiki/List_of_reported_UFO_sightings

[121] Though he is deceased, his website remains: http://www.science-frontiers.com/sourcebk.htm

peculiar and seem to defy conventional explanation. One could say that the described events were either reported erroneously or that if more information was available, the incidents would not be so mysterious. This may be true, of course, given the "cold case" nature of older reports but the descriptions exist as fodder for wonder and imagination. The mysterious reports related by Corliss that fall into the celestial category include oddly behaving lights and formations of lights in the air and even seen on the Moon, dimensional bodies traversing the sky, crossing in front of the sun, moving oddly and presenting an unnatural appearance. The observing public would see and report these incidents to newspapers and journals, which were always seeking new information about nature's various unusual behaviors. The rise of human aviation and increasing interest in the sky and beyond led to accelerating the rise of a genre of literature, science fiction, which can be seen becoming popular in the works of Jules Verne and early writers influenced by the industrial and scientific revolutions, which had been ongoing for some time. Science fiction, of course, could be identified in writings going back centuries, but it was always a backwater of literature and informed speculation until technology became more prominent.

Verne's imagination saw the development of large "airships" that would travel the skies under wind and propeller power. The vehicles were, by today's standards, awkward and seemed unlikely to fly at all with rudders, cables, fins, and flapping wings arranged in impractical fashion but visually exciting to observe. Verne's imaginings became impressed in the collective public mind. This was how airships of the future should look, according to Verne and those inspired by him from the beginnings of his writings in the 1860s and on.

In November 1896, residents of northern California reported seeing strange aerial vehicles, airships, in the first large wave of reports of apparent unidentified flying objects.[122] There was much speculation as to the origin of the airships, most revolving around the activities of mysterious inventors. Yet some wondered if there was another, more exotic, explanation. Newspapers emphasized the mystery with sensational headlines (recall this was the era of "yellow journalism" when the press often merged fact with speculation for increased readership). Airships were described as "soaring between Heaven and Earth," [123]

---

[122] Extensive press coverage from California papers in personal files.
[123] San Francisco Call, November 23, 1896.

the "Light That Never Touches Land or Sea," [124] "Mars and Venus Under Suspicion." [125] This latter suggested that mistaken observations of Mars and Venus in the sky could have accounted for reports but headlines like this can be read as suggesting other planets were in the mix of discussion. One paper suggested that a Colonel H. G. Shaw encountered beings from Mars in the form of a landed airship and strange beings.[126] Mars was the object of much speculation as being the home of an intelligent civilization. Percival Lowell just a few years earlier had published a book about canals on Mars being the product of intelligence.[127] So one can see the beginnings of connecting the mass reporting of sightings of mysterious aerial objects with the activities of beings from other worlds.

1897 saw a second, even larger wave of mysterious airships reports across the U.S. Again, more Verne-type aircraft, bright lights that were attributed to being airship searchlights scanning the terrain, and considerably more wild speculation about mysterious inventors and other planets being responsible. It is very likely that Venus, very prominent in the sky that spring, was the actual source of most "searchlight" reports. Oddly, one part of the country didn't have airship reports but "Edison Electric Balloons." New Englanders believed that the bright light in the west was a beacon hoisted over Edison's central New York manufacturing plant to advertise a new communications method.[128] And the lingering talk of other planets remained. One paper said that scientists felt something was "out of doors these nights," and that "these may be visitors from Mars...." [129] As aerial technology continued to advance, the mystery airships became "mystery aeroplanes" through the first decade of the 20th century. The Wright Brothers attained powered flight in 1903, fueling the perceived reality of the unidentified aerial sightings as being due to unknown inventors competing with the Wrights. Strong interest in intelligent life on Mars continued during this time and remained an echo in the background while speculations about the unknowns and inventors grew to a peak in 1909. In England during the spring, New Zealand in our summer (their winter) and

---

[124] San Francisco Examiner, November 24, 1896.

[125] San Francisco Chronicle, November 25, 1896.

[126] Stockton CA Daily Mail, November 19, 1896.

[127] Lowell, P., Mars, Houghton, Mifflin and Company, 1895.

[128] New England press coverage in personal files.

[129] St. Louis MO Post-Dispatch, April 11, 1897.

New England in December, significant mystery aircraft flurries broke out with varying causes postulated.[130] In England, it was thought that Germans were responsible. New Zealand wasn't quite sure what was behind their activity and New England had a mystery inventor, Wallace Tillinghast, thought to be responsible but proven to be grounded while reports filtered in to newspapers. The year before World War One saw England having an intense outbreak of unknown aircraft in early 1913, thought to be due to German Zeppelins. World War One dawned in 1914 with an outbreak of mysterious airplanes in South Africa. Such reports sprouted in various locations throughout the war, causing speculation about the effect of war nerves on viewing strange objects in the sky. Wonderment about visitations from space was subdued during those years with concerns over wartime issues dominant.

At the end of the war, society could relax again and technology advanced further with help from the development and evolution of the war machine. Science fiction became an increasing source of entertainment in literature, fueling the pulp magazine industry with fantastic tales of space travel and other worlds. While a wide variety of imagery of these possibilities were brought to life on the covers of the magazines, the imagined space ships in particular were beginning to develop in the way the modern world wanted to see them. Amazing streamlined machines without the fins and rudders of the past dazzled young readers of the 1920s-1930s, impressing upon them how spacecraft might eventually appear. Some examples of the spacecraft speculations can be found on many issues of science fiction pulp cover art and books.[131] Many of the depictions show sleek, disc-shaped craft marauding through the Earth's atmosphere and outer space. Some of the images are virtually indistinguishable from reports of modern UFO sightings. It makes one wonder if the current understanding of flying saucers from other planets comes from the observation of real objects visiting the Earth as observed from 1947 onward, or if that understanding comes from man's imagination of future space vehicles as evident during the Jazz Age of the 1920s and the 1930s Depression era, as undeniably illustrated in early science fiction literature.

Another significant boost to the increasing impact of taking seriously the possibility of extraterrestrial intelligence visiting the Earth came as a broadcast on October 30, 1938 with Orson Welles' "War of the Worlds"

---

[130] Substantial press coverage in each of these areas in personal files.

[131] http://www.ufopop.org/main-page1.htm

drama. Merely hearing talk on the radio of a Martian invasion, though fictional, was enough to throw thousands of inattentive listeners into a panic, believing it actually happened. Science fiction was no longer ridiculous speculation to people but was becoming a potential peek into the future.

The influence of science fiction in molding imaginations, and sometimes reality, with ongoing advanced technological developments inspired by those fictional tales, increased further as World War Two came upon the world. Towards the end of the war, we saw rockets begin to be used practically, albeit destructively. Also, towards the later part of the war, a peculiar phenomenon nicknamed "Foo-Fighters"[132] plagued night fighter pilots and bomber formations over Europe and the Pacific. They were small, roundish objects, seeming to behave with intelligent movements but being entirely non-destructive. Each opponent thought they were secret weapons of the other side or an odd natural phenomenon. Reports diminished with the end of the war and were never fully resolved. In the summer of 1946, mysterious "Ghost Rockets" were seen in various parts of Europe, mainly Scandinavia.[133] They were likely mostly due to Soviet rocket testing after capturing German rocket scientists but they, like the Foo-Fighters, were presented as a mystery to the world. It is reasonable to think that the publicity of both Foo-Fighters and Ghost Rockets in the previous two years set the stage for the beginning of the flying saucer era of aerial phenomena reporting in 1947. Neither phenomenon could generate public attention in a large way, probably because both were subject to wartime (in the case of Foo-Fighters) and political (in the case of Ghost Rockets) censorship and didn't translate well enough in geographic extent and detail to satisfy the curious average person.

~

Kenneth Arnold, flying a private aircraft, said he spotted nine odd objects flying over the Cascades Mountains of the Pacific Northwest on June 24, 1947. The American press had given serious attention to this report over other occasional sightings of aerial objects in the previous several years.[134] Why this was so is the subject of speculation but the

---

[132] American Legion Magazine, December 1945.

[133] Numerous examples of US press coverage from July to September 1946.

[134] First reported in US west coast press on June 25, 1947 and nationwide by June 26th.

timing, for whatever reason, was perfect. While some saucer reports were evident in other countries, this was largely a U.S. phenomenon. The public was ready for a new, exciting interest and flying saucers were it. Hundreds of sightings occurred, and reports were dutifully passed along in newspapers, fueling yet more interest and drawing more attention. At first, flying saucers reports were seen mainly as some sort of secret devices from a foreign power, the most likely candidate being the Soviet Union. As the reports continued for several years, evidence for this connection was elusive. Many of the saucer reports were very detailed and related characteristics that were beyond the abilities of then-current military and aviation engineering. Many U.S. military officers as much as said so in formerly classified government documents released through the Freedom of Information Act (5 U.S.C, Sec. 552). Staffers of Project Sign, the Air Force's first official exploration of saucers, wrote a report in 1948, under the heading "Estimate of the Situation," daring to suggest these objects could be interplanetary but the report was never adopted as policy.[135] With the fading influence of secret weapons as an explanation, something the military couldn't demonstrate to the satisfaction of the U.S. public, thoughts about the origin of flying saucers were thrown wide open. 1948 saw a pilot, Thomas Mantell, killed in an alleged saucer encounter and, later in the summer, an airliner's encounter with a strange object was openly compared to something out of Buck Rogers, a science fiction hero.[136] A solid connection between outer space aliens and flying saucers was building.

At the end of 1949, *True Magazine*, published in New York, released an article by Major Donald Keyhoe, a colleague of Charles Lindbergh, announcing his view that flying saucers were real and from outer space, based upon three years of reports and internal conversations with government officials. [137]A short time later, in March 1950, a saucer wave broke in the U.S., and, coincident with this, an outbreak of sightings also occurred in Europe. The hole left by the failure of the early secret weapon hypothesis as the explanation for the phenomenon was gaping and needed to be filled. In both cases, space intelligence was cited as a distinct possibility though officialdom was not so convinced, at

---

[135] This report remains unavailable but the document was reported as existing by Captain Edward Ruppelt of the Air Force's Project Blue Book and Major Dewey Fournet, a Blue Book liaison officer at the Pentagon.

[136] Chiles-Whitted incident, July 24, 1948.

[137] True Magazine, January 1950.

least publicly. It was a satisfying possibility for an alarmed population, though not necessarily a proven one. But that didn't matter. From this point on, the linkage of flying saucers to possible life in the universe was complete and dominated the debate for decades. As many variations on this theme were developed as there were people engaged in these discussions, from the hyper-religious to the relatively conservative idea of the presence of extraterrestrials without overt involvement or contact with Earth.

Government maintained a negative position while an assortment of prominent individuals spoke out. While, in 1950, saucer reports seemed to respond to publicity on the ground, namely the Keyhoe True article, this happened again in 1952. Life Magazine published a decidedly pro-saucer article, asking "Have We Visitors From Outer Space?"[138] This was a very dramatic escalation in support for the life-in-space advocates as Life Magazine was influential and had a large circulation. Probably not coincidentally, sightings rose to the point of near national panic, culminating in reports of radar tracking of unknown objects over Washington, D.C. The U.S. Air Force felt it necessary to defuse the idea that aliens were here for the simple reason that such speculation would cast doubt on the defensive abilities of the military and that this speculation was circumstantial and not proven. A press conference was held on July 29 by the Air Force,[139] cooling the panic but not eliminating the reporting of saucers. Aliens were firmly in people's thoughts whenever the topic was raised, as declarations from authority were not enough to discourage such a sensational concept.

1950 saw the first serious intermixing of extraterrestrial intelligence into the flying saucer mix, and, to a lesser extent, mention of extraterrestrial beings. 1954 saw a much greater intermixing of saucer beings, not so much this time in the U.S. as in Europe. A wave of "little man" reports swept the continent, especially France.[140] Landed UFOs released aliens interacting with the landscape, allegedly taking physical samples and doing what scientists would do if they were on another planet. This has the appearance of an increasing and systematic investigation of the human race. European press screamed headlines about invasion from other worlds, particularly Mars, which, since the days of Percival Lowell, was still thought to harbor intelligent life. The question is, was it real?

---

[138] Life Magazine, April 7, 1952.

[139] 32-page transcript in personal files.

[140] Extensive press coverage in world press from September to December 1954.

Reports of aliens coming even closer to, and interacting with humans, came about as the 1950s progressed with the rise of the contactee movement. Percipients advertised themselves as middlemen with aliens, relating space brother philosophy, songs and poems, and urgent messages to disarm from atomic warfare. This is not unlike what films and television were airing as entertainment throughout this era. This does raise a curious question, though.

The activity of flying saucers and their occupants seems to be almost as much a fulfillment of the expectations of how humans think aliens should behave as opposed to real visitations of alien intelligence. For example, instead of modern images of sleek, metallic interplanetary vehicles that have persisted since 1947, the 1897 objects that were the flying saucers of their day were clunky, awkward vehicles that conformed more to the image of what advanced technology should look like in the Victorian minds' eye. Some even thought they traveled from Mars, as if somehow fins and propellers would aid moving in a vacuum.

The progression of flying saucer reports went from being seen streaking across the sky in 1947 to closer, more detailed views in 1950. Then the observations became more technically established with the use of radar in 1952, followed by landings in 1954 along with seeing creatures from afar. This was followed by claims of contact and verbal exchanges. Not all of this is legitimate, of course, but it is a trend of the reports in general. What would logically follow? A probing extraterrestrial civilization might want to tinker physically with humans to see how they tick perhaps? And that's exactly what happened. Beginning in the 1960s, witnesses began to report being abducted by aliens. Characteristic of this is the experience of Barney and Betty Hill, a story much retold in UFO literature.[141] They were followed by a multitude of claimants of abduction and physical probing to varying degrees. In an escalating stairway of strangeness, one might next expect claims of humans' being the product of alien interaction. This, too, has come about with the discussion of "hybrid" people, a mix of alien and man and some outright claiming they are aliens.

Mysteries remain, but, in general, were flying saucers influencing man's culture, or was man's culture influencing flying saucers?

---

[141] Fuller, John G., *The Interrupted Journey*, 1966.

Printed in September 2021
by Rotomail Italia S.p.A., Vignate (MI) - Italy